THE
SUMNER
STORY

THE SUMNER STORY

*Capturing Our History
Preserving Our Legacy*

Volume I, First Edition

WILMA F. BONNER

SANDRA E. FREELAIN

DWIGHT D. HENDERSON

JOHNNIEQUE B. LOVE

EUGENE M. WILLIAMS

EDITED BY WILMA F. BONNER

NEW YORK

THE SUMNER STORY

Capturing Our History Preserving Our Legacy

Volume I, First Edition

by Wilma F. Bonner, Sandra E. Freelain, Dwight D. Henderson,
Johnnieque B. Love, Eugene M. Williams

ISBN 978-1-60037-780-8 (paperback)
ISBN 978-1-60037-781-5 (hardcover)
Library of Congress Control Number: 2010928885

Published by:

MORGAN JAMES PUBLISHING, LLC
1225 Franklin Ave. Ste 325
Garden City, NY 11530-1693
Toll Free 800-485-4943
www.MorganJamesPublishing.com

Interior Design by:
Bonnie Bushman
bbushman@bresnan.net

In an effort to support local communities, raise awareness and funds, Morgan James Publishing donates one percent of all book sales for the life of each book to Habitat for Humanity.
Get involved today, visit **www.HelpHabitatForHumanity.org.**

WORDS ABOUT THE BOOK...

This story of Sumner High School in Kansas City, Kansas is a very welcome addition to the education literature. It provides a solid history lesson on effective schooling for blacks in that city for five generations, more than seventy years. It is rich with comments and assessments from graduates who credit their sound learning base at Sumner for their subsequent successes in higher education, in negotiating the ways in the world, and in the career ladders that they chose. Cognitive mastery was their core; that, coupled with infusions of proper values and attitudes, made Sumner's graduates competent and capable as they moved into adult life. Every Kansas school and library should add this book to their collection. Today's students need to understand the value of education, motivation, and school related connections to their lives and future well being. Kansans should be quite proud of Sumner High School and its graduates. This book helps to fill the void that exists regarding the successful education of blacks in this nation, despite the imposed limitations of legal racial segregation.

Faustine C. Jones-Wilson, Ed.D.
Professor Emerita Howard University
Washington, D.C.

Contemporary educators, policymakers and parents have much to learn from The Sumner Story about school quality, community cohesiveness and -- in a word -- excellence! Sumner High School was staffed with exceptionally credentialed principals and teachers who possessed superior knowledge about the education and socialization of children and youth. These legendary educators' strategic equations yielded consistent fruit -- generations of graduates who had an intellectual competitive edge and a moral compass which enabled them to be professionally successful, independent and proud, and contributing citizens in their communities despite Jim Crow and its vestiges. My parents are graduates of the famed Sumner

High School and Dunbar High School (Washington, DC). Growing up I was regaled with stories about Sumner and Dunbar and the lessons my parents learned from their teachers. More than a historical tome, this research volume affirms what can and should be achieved in our nation's schools.

Leslie T. Fenwick, Ph.D.
Dean, School of Education, Howard University
Washington, D.C

The writers touch on intangible benefits of the Sumner experience, such as the clear and present caring and personal sacrifice of teachers and administrators; the sense of togetherness – due to both internal and external prompts – felt by the students; and the pride of the whole community in the beauty of the school. They explore carefully the tangible factors impacting the school's prolonged success: the faculty, curricula, co-curricular programs, and evidence of high standards and expectations. Can students be admonished to "BE THE BEST" outside of a segregated setting? Certainly, the Sumner organizing principle, that "Education is serious business – it is imperative!" could be in place in an integrated setting – but would the students of color know they were included? How can the success of Sumner and the other historically segregated schools that are studied, be resurrected for today's students?...All who care about the highest quality of public education for today's African American students should thoroughly digest this powerful study of Sumner – and act upon it!

Ramona H. Edelin, Ph. D.
Executive Director, D.C. Public Charter School Association
Washington, D.C.

DEDICATION

The Sumner Story is dedicated to the founders, teachers, administrators, and total school community who set in place and carried out a vision and philosophy that resulted in continuous learning and development for all students who graced the halls of Sumner High School during its seven decades of existence

...and to

the many students who grew intellectually, physically, and emotionally to become leaders and productive citizens of our nation and the world.

Acknowledgments

To Chester ('49) and Lilli Owens ('53) who have been a team in sharing the Sumner story through lectures, tours, and continuous one-on-one conversations, we hope that your knowledge of history and passion for the community lives on in the lives of those you've touched.

To Beckwith ('56) and Gwen Horton ('56), whose leadership and support have been so critical to the success of this project, we give you the credit and accolades you so justly deserve. Although you consistently told us you wanted to remain in the background, we see this acknowledgement as nonnegotiable.

To the Class of 1930 and the Sumner High School Alumni Association, we salute your efforts in organizing and establishing the Sumner High School Alumni Association. You have secured many of our archival documents, protecting and preserving them in the Kansas Collection of the Spencer Research Library at the University of Kansas.

To the Spencer Research Library's Kansas Collection at the University of Kansas, we are indebted to preservation and conservation of the Sumner High School Collection. Established in 1986 by donations from past faculty, students, and the Sumner Class of 1930, this collection was among the earliest research materials acquired through the systematic African-American collecting program, which continues to be an active part of the Kansas Collection. By having these materials preserved in the Kansas Collection, Sumner High School's impressive contributions to the history of education are now a part of the region's permanent historical record. Special commendations go to Sheryl Williams, curator, and Deborah Dandridge, field archivist.

———————————

To William Walker, the writing team thanks you for your technological expertise and look forward to learning about your continued development and advancement in the field.

———————————

To Dennis Lawrence, the authors extend appreciation for thorough and balanced documentation of the Sumner history in your award-winning dissertation, *The Impact of Local, State and Federal Government Decisions on the Segregation and Subsequent Integration of Sumner High School in Kansas City, Kansas*, 1997. This narrative proved to be an invaluable asset to the completion of our story.

———————————

To the many alumni, who responded to the survey, answered our phone calls, and participated in our information-gathering sessions, we appreciate your part of the story!

FOREWORD

Citadel of Learning and Harvard of the Midwest are two of the many names that can be used to describe Sumner High School in Kansas City, Kansas. The history of Sumner High School is a magnificent story of an institution born out of an unfortunate racial incident that occurred in 1904. As a result, Sumner High School became the only all African-American high school in the state of Kansas by law. From its inception, the black community was committed to the principles of excellence.

Classroom instructors were carefully selected and many possessed advanced educational degrees. Sumner's record of academic achievement is phenomenal. In every decade of its existence, there were graduates who became Phi Beta Kappans, notable scholars, leaders, and upstanding citizens who attribute their success to the foundation they received at Sumner.

The demographics of the school community consisted of students who were the offspring of citizens from every walk of life - from laborers to physicians. These citizens led busy, honest lives, and most were devoted congregants in the many churches throughout this African-American community. Although Sumner High School was closed in 1978, its legacy is still alive and well.

The torch of pride and educational excellence has been passed on to the children of the Sumner Spartans who carry on the traditions that were laid many years ago. It is hoped that information contained in this story will be used as a roadmap by educators, communities, and governmental entities for reaching higher educational goals.

The question arises, "Will those standards of excellence and levels of success found in the legacy of Sumner High School ever be duplicated?"

— Chester C. Owens, Jr. (Class of 1949)

TABLE OF CONTENTS

Our story must be told and never allowed to die. Future generations must know about the great Sumner High School of Kansas City, Kansas.

— Lilli A. Yates Owens, Class of 1953

LIST OF PHOTOGRAPHS

LIST OF TABLES

CHAPTER ONE

INTRODUCTION

We had a gold mine and didn't realize it until it was taken away from us.

— Beverly J. Caruthers Thompson, Class of 1954

For the first three-quarters of the twentieth century, in the heart of the nation, there thrived a safe haven that nurtured great aspirations of thousands of African-American youth and their families; it was called Sumner High School. Located in the northeast corner of Kansas City, Kansas, this bastion of learning climaxed the last three years of public education for approximately fourteen thousand students over a period of seven decades. Although unique to Kansas City, Sumner was not unlike a significant number of segregated high schools across the nation that served the dual function of a safe harbor for academic excellence and a strategic bridge to adulthood for African-American students. Whether students joined the armed services, married and began families, traveled abroad, entered the workforce, or continued their studies in colleges or vocational schools, their high school years were pivotal in readying them to enter a demanding and diverse world.

In a socially and economically segregated nation, black students who had a "Sumner-like" experience were very fortunate, because their schools served as clear windows and powerful springboards to promising possibilities of the future. The high expectations, relentless demands, and keen competition fostered in such hallowed institutions signaled a world of hard knocks, compromises, and closed doors. But they also cultivated the vision and resilience needed to overcome and succeed in that world. As both predictors and portals, Sumner and other black high schools left indelible imprints on the lives of their graduates as they journeyed forward. The foresight and efforts of the Sumner faculty to facilitate a comprehensive preparation, not for a special few, but for the masses of students who had a wide array of interests and inclinations will be remembered and cherished for a lifetime.

Students achieved at higher levels with black teachers. The athletic program was superbly managed and rated tops in the U.S.A. The cosmetology program, instructed by Ms. Rosemary Daniels, was outstanding! The instrumental music, vocal music and art departments educated the students effectively for world wide contributions. Woodwork, welding, and machine shop courses produced careers and reading ready citizens.

— Donald S. Jefferson, Class of 1946

The critical role that public high schools played in building strong and confident African Americans cannot be refuted or trivialized in light of the leaders and responsible citizenry they produced. Victories came in spite of insidious racial discrimination, economic uncertainty, and social disequilibrium that plagued the country and permeated the schools. When ineptitude, failure, and subsistence were mainstream America's expectations for its minority populations, black segregated high schools painted another picture. They projected mastery, hope, and high standards of living for their students. They served as lighthouses for safe and prosperous passage into a new era. These schools continued the tasks of removing post slavery chains; they helped lessen fears and low self-esteem from the hearts and minds of young men and women who entered their doors. Sumner, and other black segregated high schools on its par, promoted and nurtured self-confidence, courage, dormant talent, and potential for thousands of African Americans.

INTENT

At a time of national concern over the ongoing achievement gap between blacks and whites, the shifting of minority standing of blacks in American demographics, and growing displacement of blacks in the workplace, the stories of success attributable to segregated high schools of the past must be told by their many beneficiaries. And indeed, the voices of Sumner alumni ring clear the gratitude and understanding of the fights and feats on their behalf. Their impressions and memories are deeply embedded and remain as vibrant today as they were decades ago.

The superintendent [of the Kansas City, Kansas, public schools] verbalized several times in my hearing a clear message that you people were different and inferior. In retrospect, what society meant as a burden turned into a blessing—

segregation kept us close, the Superintendent kept us focused, and economics kept us trying to prepare ourselves for a better future.

— Janet L. Rogers Morgan, Class of 1957

Although our story focuses on the legacy of "Dear Ole Sumner High" in Wyandotte County, Kansas, the intent of this book is to acknowledge jubilantly and factually the spirit, character, and tenacity of educators, parents, and cities and towns across the country who built communities of black achievers. For the most part, between 1905 and 1978, our parents and teachers abandoned initial desires of their ancestors to return to the motherland from which they had been stolen. Rather, they were determined to better their own lives and those of their children by establishing claims of permanent residency, equality, and leadership in this country. It was through public schools such as Sumner that major inroads were made on this side of the Atlantic Ocean to affirm that the quality of life could be enhanced, re-envisaged, and realized for the African American. Our parents and teachers lovingly and untiringly set the stage for successive generations to take their respective places at every level in American society and the world. In addition to their guidance, the school curricula were strong and the co-curricular activities went far beyond the basics to ensure students had broad and meaningful exposures.

The teachers were the best ... In the spring of 1952, we performed The Mikado, an operetta. Mr. Isaiah D. Ruffin, the teacher, actually ordered the score for vocals and instrumentals from New York. He had to have the rights to perform this music. He then ordered the actual costumes from New York. This operetta was a professional performance by high school students.

— Laleta Schuler Jones, Class of 1955

At Sumner, adults shouldered their responsibility for "nation rebuilding." They were notably committed to ensuring that all students understood the connection between a high-quality education and ultimate success in life. All of the adults at Sumner—teachers, administrators, and support staff—were unrelenting in helping students understand that literacy (listening, speaking, reading, and writing) and numeracy (computing and manipulating numbers) were the primary means for commerce and communication. Their goal was to prepare every student to "Be the

Best," a theme carried over from the feeder junior high school, Northeast. Dignity, integrity, and respect for others provided texture for the setting in which literacy and numeracy were taught. It is the intent of this story to affirm the impact of these concerted efforts on its individual and collective graduates and, in large measure, to inspire successive generations to do the same.

> *The principal strength of the program resides in the many dedicated and capable faculty members who strive to provide meaningful educational experiences for their pupils … Sumner High School has had a proud history and many persons on the staff work diligently to retain elements of this heritage and to regain other aspects of it.*

> — Taken from the North Central Association and Kansas State Department of Education Evaluation Report, March 1969

A second intent of this story, as the title indicates, is to consider measures that can be taken to preserve and build upon the legacy of Sumner and other schools across this nation that were similar to Sumner. Through the thoughts and experiences that are shared, it is hoped that there will be a better understanding of why and how certain strategies prevalent during the Sumner days need to be replicated to stimulate and support educational institutions that serve black youth today. Values, attitudes, practices, and curricula of the past will be examined through the lens of the present. Ideally, these reflections will add to a greater body of knowledge on how African-Americans in this country survived the past, are overcoming the present, and will excel in the future. The common threads of public school strides are seen by the writers and their fellow Sumnerians as causes to celebrate and replicate, in part or whole, in schools of today.

> *I would choose to be educated at Sumner [again] because we had teachers who cared about educating students [lifelong learning]. I would want all African-American children to have the same Sumner experience.*

> — Johnnie M. Wooten, Class of 1958

> *I am thankful that I had the opportunity to attend Sumner High School. I was taught that I had value and that I could be somebody if I made wise decisions. Sumner will always be special for me.*

> — Bernice Long Johnson, Class of 1958

Finally, some recounts in *The Sumner Story* present personal anecdotes of former students to add texture and flavor; they help the reader gain an understanding or evoke memories of the people, times, and events that factored into Sumner's rich legacy.

> *My husband graduated from Bonner Springs High School; but he is a wannabe Sumnerite. He said that Bonner "dudes" would come to town on weekends just to be in the midst of cool Sumnerites and even listened to the request show on KPRS [radio show] going out for the cool guys and dolls of Sumner High School.*
>
> — Judy Dangerfield, Sumner Class of 1965;
> daughter of Katharine Charleston Hadley, Class of 1944

A number of students were precocious in their appreciation of the high expectations teachers set for them; they understood the value of their education. Although there is frivolity in the following excerpt from a feature article in the school newspaper, the respect for rigor is clear.

> *The third hour chemistry class is composed of seventeen true Sumnerites, for we were the second class in the building to have one hundred per cent subscription to the* Sumner Courier, *and during the six weeks we had only one case of tardiness.*

Figure 1.1 Chemistry Lab 1926

You should very grateful be,
To us who study chemistry,
We tell you water's H2O,
And lots of things you'd never know,
We'll starve before we rise to fame,
But we'll keep going just the same.
We'll get our share of the fun no doubt,
From flunking high school students out.

The teacher watches in the lab,
To make us work instead of gab.
We know our C.U. from F. E.,
And H.B.R. from T.N.T.
We're studying atoms and molecules,
And also formulas and rules.
You'd be lucky to get a "three,"
If you should study chemistry.

(Taken from the *Sumner Courier*, published by Sumner High School, November 15, 1921.)

Perhaps the Sumner poem titled "Remember," which was submitted to the story writers by Shirley Webster Howard, Class of 1952, best summarizes our compulsions to tell Sumner's story.

Remember the times you've had here,
Remember when you're away,
Remember the friends you've made here,
And don't forget to come back some day.
Remember the halls and classrooms,
Remember your teachers too,
For you belong to Sumner,
And Sumner belongs to you.

MOTIVATION

On December 7, 1977, Dr. Walter L. Davies, assistant superintendent for instruction in the Kansas City, Kansas, public schools, met with students, parents, and faculty to inform them that Sumner High School would be closed as an open enrollment public high school effective May 1978. By decree from the Kansas City, Kansas Public School Board of Education, which was ordered by the U.S. District Court to integrate the school, Sumner High School became Sumner Academy of Arts and Sciences. The school reopened in September 1978 as a magnet school for high-achieving students. Although the expectations of high moral standing and academic achievement were maintained, and debatably heightened as hallmarks of the academy, accessibility to Sumner became exclusive.

They're calling it a magnet school, but the concept is the same as we operated over the years. I've always called Sumner a citadel of learning because that's what it was.

— opined Mr. S. H. Thompson, principal from 1951–1972.
Kansas City Times, May 29, 1978

Beginning in August 1978, students were admitted through a competitive enrollment process. For acceptance, students were required to be in the top 50 percent of their class, not have any grades below a 3 (C) on their report cards, and maintain a grade point average of 2.5 or higher to remain enrolled. Sumner had been transformed into a select school, accommodating the most academically accomplished students in grades nine through twelve, who came from all parts of the city.

To the dismay of many city residents and Sumner alumni who had settled in different places across the nation, enrollment dramatically changed from a predominately African-American majority. When the doors initially reopened, 41 percent of the 620 students were black, and 55 percent were white. As of the summer of 2008, demographics reflected a student body of 1,062 students: 42 percent black, 31 percent white, 19 percent Hispanic/Latin American, 7 percent Asian, and less than 1 percent Native American. Since the first day of Sumner Academy, the repercussions of closing the lone black high school have been most painfully felt by families living in close proximity to the school whose children do not qualify for admission. The "transformational" move of Sumner added to the slow demise of feeder elementary and junior high schools and brought blight to a community that had already begun to disintegrate. The new academy helped to seal the relocation of the community's hub to outlying places that were virtually unknown to alumni from the classes of 1905–1970. For sure, it marked the end of a unique social, educational, and economic era in the northeast quadrant of the city.

METHOD

Although Sumner alumni have historically held individual class reunions at five-year intervals to rekindle memories and friendships among classmates, the new magnet school gave birth to a palpable need to safeguard the legacy of the original Sumner High School aggregate of classes. To address the groundswell specifically, a regional Sumner Alumni Association meeting was held in 1993 to determine if alumni would be inclined to return to celebrate their alma mater in a national convention. It was a clear consensus that they would. The association brought the concept to fruition by holding the first all-school convention in the summer of 1995. As an outgrowth of its overwhelming success, the all-school reunion was repeated in the summers of 2000 and 2005; it is being planned again for 2010. During the third reunion, there was a compelling sentiment for the story of Sumner and its mighty Spartans to be documented formally by Sumnerites. Prior to the final session of that 2005 reunion, the association endorsed the writing of *The Sumner Story*. A financial backer was identified to support the project, a team comprised of five "writing members" was formed to outline a blueprint and lay the groundwork for the effort, and a strategy was agreed on to move forward.

The writing team met and developed a four-page survey, which was mailed in February of 2006 to over six hundred active participants in the Sumner Alumni Association and to other alumni whose addresses could be found. The survey was designed to glean experiences at Sumner that had an impact on the lives of its students after high school. It was intended to help gain perspective on the guidance and preparation students received at a "separate but equal" school. Finally, the survey was crafted to help acknowledge the scholarship, love, and care that teachers, administrators, and staff gave to propel thousands of youth far beyond the home of the Spartans, far beyond the land of burnt orange and black. The writing team also convened focus groups in Kansas City, Kansas, and in Washington, D.C., to capture oral accounts of alumni's experiences. To add depth and a spirit of inclusivity, responses from the survey and the focus groups are interwoven throughout this story.

This book is divided into distinct chapters, aligned with the survey instrument, which address different aspects of the Sumner experience. Chapter 2 provides historical data drawn from a variety of primary and secondary sources that highlight the social, economic, and political landscapes during the life of the school. The historical backdrop shows the connection and/or isolation of Sumner to local, national, and world events. Chapter 3 is devoted to the origins and development of Sumner High in Kansas City, Kansas. Chapters 4 and 5 offer insight into the legacy of Sumner as revealed by over a hundred Spartan alumni who responded to the survey and three hundred more who participated in the Sumner Alumni Association's History and Archival Committee's project, Family Histories. Information has also been included from anecdotes shared in class reunions, personal collections of alumni, news articles, and other Sumner and Kansas memorabilia found in the Sumner High School Collection of the University of Kansas Kenneth Spencer Research Library. Specifically, chapter 4, "What Kept Sumner Together," provides a mosaic of curricula, co-curricular activities, people, and practices that evolved into an institutional masterpiece. Chapter 5, "Memories, Reflections, and Perspectives," is comprised of firsthand memories of alumni that reveal how it was "back in the day." Chapter 6, "Fruit Yielded," catapults the reader into the lives of graduates decades and scores after their Sumner experience. The chapter provides limited information on what happened to specific individuals, but nuances the fates of thousands. Finally, chapter 7, "Other Portals to Success," highlights nine high schools across the country that served as bastions of excellence for black students, as did Sumner.

In addition to recounts of what transpired in society and in students' personal lives during their enrollment at Sumner, presented in italics, each chapter attempts to capture perceptions of the role the school played in supporting students' cognitive, social, and emotional development. The survey, which serves as a frame for telling the story, is presented here.

Please share this questionnaire with other Spartans!!

SUMNER WRITING PROJECT QUESTIONNAIRE

Capturing Our History / Preserving our Legacy

Name _____ Class of 19_____

PLEASE NOTE: Your responses are greatly appreciated and will contribute to a lasting document that brings to life the legacy of Sumner High! Be mindful that this questionnaire covers a broad range of topics. Choose only those that you feel comfortable in addressing. Don't hesitate to add more pages if you need additional space to capture your memories. If you prefer an electronic copy to provide your responses, please e-mail j.b.love@att.net or jlove1@umd.edu

I. DEMOGRAPHICS (ABOUT YOU)

Gender: ❑ Male ❑ Female

What years did you attend Sumner? ❑ '20s ❑ '30s ❑ '40s ❑ '50s ❑ '60s ❑ '70s

What elementary school(s) did you attend? _____

What junior high school did you attend? _____

Did you ❑ walk or ❑ ride to school?

If you rode, did you come by ❑ bus or ❑ car?

Did you ❑ own or ❑ have ready access to a car?

What is your highest level of formal education?

❑ High School   ❑ Associate's Degree   ❑ Bachelor's Degree
❑ Master's Degree   ❑ Doctorate's Degree   ❑ Juris Doctorate
❑ Medical Degree   ❑ professional license(s) _____
❑ other _____

What is the highest level of formal education of each of your children? (Specify the number of children for each category.)___High School Diploma ___Associate's Degree ___Bachelor's Degree ___Master's Degree ___Doctorate ___Juris Doctorate ___Medical Degree ___professional license(s)_____ ___other _____

How many generations of your family attended Sumner? _____Generations

II. Reflections on the Times (ABOUT ISSUES, EVENTS, AND CHALLENGES)

What were some of the issues or major events (in our community, nation, world) that impacted you directly during your enrollment in Sumner?

❑ Segregation   ❑ Great Depression   ❑ Health/Health Care
❑ World I   ❑ Employment   ❑ Local/National Politics
❑ World II   ❑ Integration   ❑ Civil Rights Movement
❑ Korean War   ❑ Violence   ❑ Economic Depression
❑ Vietnam War   ❑ Drugs   ❑ Lack of Resources
❑ Others _____

Did Sumner play a role in addressing these issues/events for you?
❑ Yes ❑ No ❑ Somewhat

If yes or somewhat, how were the issues addressed? Through:

❑ Counseling   ❑ Seminars   ❑ Social Clubs
❑ Faculty Members   ❑ Assemblies   ❑ Extra Curricular Clubs
❑ Other_____

Briefly discuss what role Sumner played in addressing the issue(s) you selected.

_____

_____

_____

What were some of the personal challenges that complicated your life most during your Spartan days?

❏ Health   ❏ Puberty/Adolescence

❏ Dating   ❏ Social Clubs (as member or non-member)

❏ Abuse   ❏ Death of Friend or Family member

❏ College Acceptance   ❏ Limited Financial Resources

❏ Poor Achievement   ❏ Participation in Sports (or nonparticipation)

❏ Relations with Teachers

❏ Other Challenges_____

Did Sumner play a role in addressing these challenges for you?

❏ Yes   ❏ No   ❏ Somewhat

How? _____

Through:

❏ Counseling   ❏ Seminars   ❏ Social Clubs

❏ Faculty Members   ❏ Assemblies   ❏ Classe

❏ Extra Curricular Clubs

❏ Others _____

Briefly discuss_____

_____

III. Reflections on Sumner (ABOUT YOUR OPINIONS)

What kept Sumner together?

❏ Staff   ❏ Integration   ❏ Superintendent

❏ Parental Support   ❏ Curricula   ❏ Academic Expectations

❏ Segregation   ❏ Community   ❏ Extra-Curricular Programs

❏ Sports Program   ❏ Social Expectations   ❏ Preparation of Faculty

❏ Others _____

Briefly discuss. _____

_____

What worked against Sumner?

❑ Segregation ❑ Superintendent ❑ Community

❑ Integration ❑ Students ❑ Curriculums

❑ Teachers ❑ Societal ills ❑ Economics

❑ Other _____

Briefly discuss. _____

_____

What other factors do you believe contribute to an understanding of the Sumner story? _____

_____

As you recall teachers, administrators, counselors, and others who had a profound and positive influence on your life, who were they, and what did you like most about them?

Person _____

What You Liked Most _____

What were the most positive influences of Sumner? _____

_____

In retrospect, were any aspects of a "wholesome" high school experience missing from Sumner? _____

_____

IV. Personal Memories and Reflections (ABOUT OVERALL FEELINGS, IMPRESSIONS)

What life lessons did you learn from Sumner? _____

_____

If you had it to do over again, would you choose to be educated at Sumner, as you remember it? ❑ Yes ❑ Maybe ❑ No

Why or Why Not? _____

If you had the option, would you want your child(ren) or grandchild(ren) to have the same or similar "Sumner" experience that you had? ❏ Yes ❏ No

Why/Why not? _____

Have you participated with your class since graduation? If so, how frequently?

❏ Optimally (every class reunion)   ❏ Frequently (most class reunions)
❏ Not Often (at least one class reunion)   ❏ Not at All (no class reunions)

What overall grades would you give Sumner in the following areas?
(1 = exemplary; 2 = very good; 3 = satisfactory; 4 = poor; 5 = unsatisfactory)

__Academics   __Athletic Program _____ __Extra-Curricular Program
__Faculty   __School Climate _____ __Facility (Bldg. Adequacy)
__9th & Washington   __Preparation for Post–High School Life
__8th & Oakland   __Other _____

V. Personal Accomplishments (ABOUT YOU, DECADES LATER)

What are your current and past occupations/lines of work?

_____

What are the occupations of each of your children?

_____

_____

_____

What are your areas of artistic expression? _____

_____

Have you published? ❏ Yes ❏ No
If so, provide the title(s) of your publication(s)? _____

Have you had any literary, dramatic, artistic, or musical works or other products copyrighted or patented? If so what are they? _____

_____

VI. International Contributions, Service, and/or Work (ABOUT INTERNATIONAL IMPACTS)

Have you been employed outside of the United States? ❑ Yes ❑ No

If so, where? _____

Briefly discuss. _____

_____

Are you multi-lingual? ❑ Yes ❑ No

What languages? _____

What languages did you study at Sumner? _____

We appreciate your time and effort in this endeavor to capture our history and preserve our legacy. Please feel free to add any comments you feel would add to the Sumner story.

_____

_____

_____

PERMISSION ACKNOWLEDGMENT

Upon consent, each respondent will be acknowledged for contributing to this work.

I, _____, do hereby __agree or __do not agree that the Sumner Alumni Association may use any or all of the information that I have provided to them.

(Signature) _____ (Date)_____

CHAPTER TWO

HISTORICAL BACKDROP

....

Teachers tried to prepare us so we would be able to cope with the outside world
— Mildred Bradley, Class of 1942

Sumner's timeline, 1905 to 1978, is a period marked by many major events in the United States and the world. Considering their impact on the school community helps illustrate the evolution of the school and the role it played in the lives of its students. For Sumner was not only a place of refuge from the realities of politics, wars, racism, and economic woes, it was also a once-in-a-lifetime experience staffed by competent and caring people. Those critical individuals helped students sort through local and world events and their ramifications. Their insights and guidance functioned as filters through which students were able to make connections and gain perspective of the world beyond themselves.

IMPACT OF WAR

The early part of the century and the first quarter of Sumner's existence saw the end of the Spanish-American War and the beginning and end of World War I. Although there are no artifacts in Sumner's archives or mention in the returned surveys of the former war, which ended seven years before Sumner opened its doors, a number of alumni addressed the influences of World War I on the school and in their personal lives. There is evidence of school assemblies, student organizations, and classroom discussions that kept students abreast of what was happening on the warfront and that encouraged patriotism. In the foreword of the 1919 *Sumner Annual*, specific inference is made to the economic and perhaps social impact of World War I on the school.

Due to the war and other handicaps Sumner has not published an annual since 1911. But from this crude beginning we expect the Seniors of the future to carry out this start made by the Class of '11. We hope the annual is here to stay and although there are many opportunities for improvements. We hope that those who follow us will have enough pride in themselves and Dear ol' Sumner to carry them out.

Chronicled in the 1921 yearbook is recognition of students who worked with the American Red Cross Society, which received the Nobel Peace Prize in 1917 for its wartime efforts. Not only did the organization minister to the wounds of injured soldiers, it also helped to keep families abreast of their warring kin through distribution of postcards, messages, and parcels. The Red Cross Society was noted for playing an instrumental role in the return of prisoners of war to their countries. Sumnerians joined the local Red Cross organization in support of these efforts. There is also note of Sumner's organized participation in the purchase of Liberty Bonds, which helped to finance World War I.

Figure 2.1

Military Honor Roll

Boys who have represented Sumner High School in the Cause for Democracy

Abernathy,	Walter	Hill	Horace	Pearson,	George
Anderson,	Lucian	Hill,	Robert	Perkins,	Van
Baldwin,	Ralph	Hegg,	Walter	Pinkard,	Wilbur
Barksdale,	Norval	Holmes,	Carl	Porter,	Charles
Bradley,	Franklin	Holmes,	Russell	Rice,	Lorenzo
Browne,	Thomas	Hope,	Elmer	Robinson,	William
Burke,	William	Hughes,	Carl	Rollins,	Earl
Butler,	Charles	Hulsey,	William	Ross,	Walter
Calloway,	Lorenzo	Jackson,	James	Rout,	John
Carroll,	Matthew	Jenkins,	Considee	Saunders,	James
Collins,	Joseph	Jennings,	Frank	Saunders,	Ora
Cooper,	James	Johnson,	Forestine	Scruggs,	Sherman
Crawford,	Howard	Lewis,	Charles	Slaughter,	Elbert
Early,	John	Lewis,	John	Smiley,	Albert
Easley,	Lawrence	Lewis,	Ward	Smith,	Riley
Elmore,	Aaron	Maddox,	Albert	Trotter,	Ray
Fields,	Ardennis	Maddux,	Philip	Tucker,	Roy
French,	Shelton	Maddux	Walter	Turner,	Charles
French,	Werdell	Manley,	Loyd	Ward,	Clarence
Fulbright,	Leon	Mansfield	Roy	Wheeler,	George
Gardener,	Earl	Marr,	Houston	Wilkerson,	Vernon
Garlington,	McKinley	Monroe,	Russell	Williams,	Clarence
Garlington,	Taylor	Morgan,	Granville	Williams,	John
Gatewood,	Alexander	Neal,	Harry	Williams,	Murlen
Graves,	Goldie	Neeley,	Albert	Wilson,	Jesse
Green,	David	Neeley,	James	Yeargen,	Arthur
Harpole,	Harvey	Neeley,	William	Gaskin,	Chester
Harris,	Mervin	Overton,	Everett	Ransom,	Payne

Excerpts from The Sumner Graduate Yearbook
Published by the Senior Class of 1919

The other significant wars during Sumner's timeline were respectively World War II (1939–1945), the Korean War (1950–1953), and the Vietnam War (1959–1975). These wars directly affected the families of students who attended Sumner, as evidenced by responses to the Sumner survey. Excerpts from "Congress of Parents and Teachers Vanguard of Education," published in the April 25, 1942, *Sumner Courier,* provides more insight into collective parents' views of the war.

The world is at war now. Never before in the history of men has there been a battle front with so long a battle line. Never before have there been so many men under arms and never have so many persons been employed in making instruments of death. United States and Kansas are just beginning to feel the need for sacrifices … Small business is giving way to war needs. The individual is sacrificed for the group. We cannot live for today alone. Tomorrow and its needs must have a definite part in all of our thinking.

Our present need may become so great that we will lose sight of a very definite need for the peace that must follow the war. A new and clear idealism must be kept before that group that assumes the after war burden. That group is in the public schools. Therefore, the schools must be adequately manned as well as warships. They must be supported financially as well as war industries. Their morale must be sustained at a high level. They must be imbued with the spirit of sacrifice that is necessary not only to win a war, but to rebuild a civilization.

Almost three-fourths of the respondents from the classes of 1939 through 1949 noted that World War II impacted them during their enrollment in Sumner. Data from Sumner enrollment records reveal that the number of male students began to rise significantly after the war. Enrollment data from 1943 to 1949 was recorded as:

Figure 2.1 Enrollment Data from 1943 – 1949

Year	Males	Females
1943 – 44	254	340
1944 – 45	281	361
1945 – 46	331	403
1946 – 47	361	406
1947 – 48	361	408
1948 – 49	395	502

Encouraging words and guidance from the faculty and formal school assemblies were cited as the primary means through which students learned to cope with the social and emotional challenges presented by the war.

The war was on but we were encouraged to move forward.

— Dorothy Harvey, Class of 1943

The issues were discussed in class. We were encouraged to share our personal experiences. I personally wrote to servicemen during World War II.

— Avon Neely Robinson, Class of 1946

In 1946, Principal John Hodge called all the male students to the auditorium and announced that they would be drafted into the U.S. Army or military service after graduation. If grades were not kept up, they would be drafted while in school. I and many others made the decision to volunteer for military duty following our graduation. I went first to Fort Leavenworth, Kansas, and then to Ft. Riley, Kansas, where I was sworn in.

— Donald S. Jefferson, Class of 1946

Then came World War II, furnishing plenty of jobs for both parents and youth at attractive wages. Jobs took parents from the home when you were ten years old. Your parents held on to the real values of life while the parents of your companions who have dropped out became victims of the passing passions brought on by the war.

— Principal John A. Hodge, Congratulatory Letter in 1948 Yearbook

We were encouraged to read broadly and be knowledgeable; persons were secured for informational assemblies.

— Janeria Franklin Phillips, Class of 1949

Two-thirds of the respondents from the classes of 1949 through 1957 noted the Korean War as being one of the challenges that confronted them. The Sumner faculty was noted consistently as being key in helping students understand the issues surrounding the war.

The Korean War was over, but there was fear of friends' enlistment in the military.

— Janet Rogers Morgan, Class of 1957

War is not noted consistently by survey respondents as a major issue until the Class of 1964. Two-thirds of the respondents from 1964 to 1973 identified the Vietnam War as a challenge that impacted them directly.

THE GREAT DEPRESSION

Another major event that impacted the entire nation was the Great Depression, which lasted from 1929 to 1937. Some of the respondents who attended school during that era noted they had a lack of resources, but it was not clear if that was the Depression's effect or just the nature of finances in moderate- to low-income families. In fact, alumni whose attendance spanned the life of the school cited a lack of resources as one of the challenges of their youth. "Economic survival" is how Frank E. Powell '46 responded to the survey question asking what aspects were missing from Sumner experiences. In his congratulatory remarks to the Class of '46, Principal John A. Hodge wrote in the 1946 yearbook,

First, you came into the world during the great depression. About the time you were trying to take your first steps there were more than 200 pupils of Sumner High School who were receiving doles from the United States government in the form of N.Y.A. checks. This was their only way of remaining in school. Your parents were in that struggle trying to hold the family together and give you your chance… Your parents have seen you through.

RACIAL SEGREGATION

Beyond any doubt, however, the main issue that was indicated by respondents as impacting their matriculation in Sumner was the issue of racial segregation.

Segregation is the separation of groups of people by custom or by law. In segregation, the mind-set of the dominant society is to separate and oppress people. For oppression to exist, it must be in the national consciousness of the dominant culture and reinforced and perpetuated by its institutions. Such segregation resulted in both negative and positive outcomes for Sumner High School. One of the starkest disadvantages was the lack of material resources in the classrooms. On the other hand, for the major part of Sumner's history, the most powerful advantage was a staff of highly educated and motivated teachers and support personnel. This included teachers, custodians, cafeteria workers, and office assistants who were relegated to work in the black community. Segregation and discrimination were the main reasons for a lack of their career options, but they served a grateful body of students.

For me segregation was a plus. Teachers exerted themselves to provide all we needed as pre-college students.

— Marian Singleton Jackson, Class of 1934

Our teachers were qualified to teach us on college level. They were concerned about the students to be able to go onto higher levels of education.

— Dorothy Johnson Pearson, Class of 1940

Sumner instilled self-confidence and pride in its students that the other institutions did not/could not. Racial pride was and is still important ... When integration became a reality, persons of means moved their children to other neighborhoods and lost interest in Sumner. The District took [many of] our quality teachers and moved them to other schools.

— Janeria M. Franklin Phillips, Class of 1949

During the time, Sumner was our only option, and it was a valuable experience. Segregation was a fact of life. Our teachers, however, told us change was coming and we should be ready!

— Dr. Abel B. Sykes Jr., Class of 1952

I expected the limitation of segregation but not to be limited by it.

— William Strickland, Class of 1953

Even though my daughter received a good high school education, she did not have the "closeness" we had in a segregated school.

— LaLeta Schuler Jones, Class of 1955

Kansas City appointed Mr. D. W. Lewis, my former principal at Douglass Grade School, Superintendent of Colored Schools. He was a role model along with other black teachers who lived in our community. Many of these teachers did not have opportunities to teach in other places. We had probably some of the best teachers in the state. We had teachers in high school with master's degrees and many were working on PhDs.

— Ambassador Delano E. Lewis, Class of 1956

Since black teachers could not teach elsewhere, Sumner ended up with highly qualified instructors.

— The Honorable Cordell D. Meeks Jr., Class of 1960

It appears that along with Sumner students, the United States grappled with the overarching issue of what should be done about segregation/integration. Even at the founding of our country, this was a critical issue: what should we do with the colored folks? In the Declaration of Independence, which set the stage for the Constitution, the Founders wrote:

We hold these truths to be self evident, that all men are created equal, that they are endowed by their Creator with certain unalienable rights, that among these are life, liberty and the pursuit of happiness.

But over a decade later, when the Constitution was adopted, slavery was still an issue. It remained a concern during the Revolutionary War, because slavery and freedom were coexisting as equal but opposite parts of the American experience.

Slavery had officially been abolished before the dawning of Sumner High School, but the reality of slavery and its offspring, "Jim Crow," was still alive and well. According to Ronald L. F. Davis, "Jim Crow became a racial slur synonymous with black, colored, or Negro in the vocabulary of many whites; and by the end of the 19th century, acts of racial discrimination toward blacks were often referred to as Jim Crow laws and practices."[1] The Jim Crow segregation laws gained significant impetus from U.S. Supreme Court rulings in the last two decades of the nineteenth century. In 1883, the Supreme Court ruled unconstitutional the Civil Rights Act of 1875. This act had stipulated that all persons were entitled to full and equal enjoyment of accommodations, advantages, facilities, and other places of public amusement.

Not long after striking down the Civil Rights Act of 1875, the Supreme Court also ruled that separate but equal was constitutional and acceptable in the *Plessy v. Ferguson* 1896 case. The Court ruled that the separate accommodations provided to blacks were equal to those provided to whites and, did not stamp the colored race with a badge of inferiority. Then, in 1899, the Supreme Court further declared in the case of *Cummings v. Richmond County Board of Education*, that since Richmond County, Georgia, had only enough money to provide a high school for whites, it need not shut down the white school in the interests of separate but equal. So, this case opened the door for the elimination of black schools in districts able to assert financial hardships. It also clearly indicated that the Court was more interested in enforcing the "separate" part of *Plessy* over the "equal" part.

Thus, when Sumner was born, there was much segregation among and around the country, which lent itself to the solution of establishing Sumner as a separate high school in Kansas City, Kansas. Segregation in public accommodations and in practically all forms of living and social activities remained prevalent until 1948.

The next noteworthy legal decision that had a far-reaching impact on the nation's practice of segregation in our school systems was *Brown v. Board of Education* in 1954. This Supreme Court decision overturned the *Plessy* decision and held that, separate was inherently unequal. It did not change society; it did, however, point the way and provided a basis for the civil rights struggle. It set in motion a highly contested mandate for school boards around the country to begin integrating all of their public education institutions.

---

1   R. L. F. Davis, "Creating Jim Crow: In-Depth Essay", http://www.jimcrowhistory.org/history/creating2.htm (accessed March 30, 2010).

The Brown case did not have an immediate social impact on the school system. I can remember one corollary impact. We had a bus company owned by blacks called the McCallop Bus Company. The McCallop buses would bring black students from other parts of Wyandotte County to Sumner. Therefore, when you started integrating, one of the casualties of that integration was the demise of the bus company. McCallop lost its clientele because after the Brown decision blacks began to attend their neighborhood schools and there was no longer a need for buses to bring black students into the previously segregated schools.

— Ambassador Delano E. Lewis, Class of 1956

But, it was more than twenty years after the *Brown v. the Topeka Board of Education* court decision that the U.S. Court Judge for the Kansas City area declared that feeder schools to Sumner and Sumner High School, itself, must be integrated. The Kansas City, Kansas School Board then decided to discontinue the school that had been established for blacks in 1905, and in effect, create a new school that would attract white citizens. In the spring of 1978, the old Sumner closed. In the fall of 1978, the new Sumner Academy emerged as a magnet high school.

CIVIL RIGHTS PROTEST MOVEMENT

Another major development that occurred during Sumner High School's timeline that impacted the segregated infrastructure of America was the civil rights protest era. Strategic protests were designed across the nation to bring attention to the fact that black people were living in America as second-class citizens. Many organizations and individuals participated in these efforts, such as Martin Luther King Jr., Stokely Carmichael, Malcolm X, the National Association for the Advancement of Colored People (NAACP), the Black Panther Party, Congress of Racial Equality (CORE), and the Student Non-Violent Coordinating Committee (SNNC). But it is generally acknowledged that the protest movement was irreversibly ignited by two incidents that occurred in 1955: Emmett Till's murder in Money, Mississippi, and Rosa Parks' refusal to give up her seat on a public bus in Montgomery, Alabama. These two critical acts set the stage for many groups and leaders to denounce segregation and its attendant Jim Crow customs that held blacks in unequal positions relative to jobs, earnings, education, public accommodations, and so on. The protest movement also set the stage for the ultimate decision by the federal judge of Kansas City, Kansas, to declare that Sumner High School and its feeder schools must be desegregated.

The protest movement was much more active across the country than it was in Kansas City, Kansas. However, on February 14, 1969, about 125 black students left Sumner High School and marched to Wyandotte High School to protest a lack of black history programs at Sumner and a perceived lack of equitable funding for the school. In his dissertation, Lawrence (1998) captured the essence and aftermath of the walkout.

> *In 1969, absenteeism at Sumner during the one day school boycott was 50%. Four days later, the Board of Education agreed to meet with the group, and the boycott of the Avenue merchants ended. The instigators of this spring of boycotts were students of Sumner High School. In a week of peaceful demonstrations, the students had forced onto the table the seminal issues of segregated schools— the right to determine curriculum, the right to equal funding, and, above all, the right to address grievances to those with the power to make changes if not amends. On the evening the boycott of Avenue merchants ended, 266 members of the Sumner High School Class of 1969 received their high school diplomas at Memorial Hall where some had sat in protest some four months earlier. Forty-three of these graduates received scholarships totaling $52,335. Of the traditional gift of the graduating class to the school, there is no record, but the legacy of the class of 1969 was etched during the winter of discontent that preceded their spring graduation.[2]*

This discontent also served as impetus for the Board of Education to pass a bond issue in 1970 that led to the construction of a new cafeteria and gymnasium at Sumner. These projects were completed before the opening of school in August 1975. So, the protest movement that swept the country eventually got to Sumner, and the Board of Education felt compelled to take some action.

---

2   D. Lawrence, "The Impact of Local, State, and Federal Government Decisions on the Segregation and Subsequent Integration of Sumner High School in Kansas City, Kansas" (dissertation, 1998), 77–94.

CHAPTER THREE

SUMNER HIGH SCHOOL'S EARLY BEGINNINGS AND EVOLUTION

And so we have come to this great Sumner High School—eager to learn; anxious to know; inquisitive enough to find out.

— Earl J. Blackmon Class of '65

CHRONOLOGY OF SUMNER HIGH SCHOOL

1886–1904	Black and white students attended Kansas City, Kansas High School, only high school in Kansas City, Kansas.
January 1901	Kansas Legislature passed General Statues; Section 6290, provided for integration of high schools.
April 12, 1904	Roy Martin, a white student, was killed by Louis Gregory, older black youth, in Kerr Park.
April 13, 1904	Kansas City, Kansas High School dismissed due to demonstration by white students and citizens.
April 14, 1904	Superintendent Pearson declared school closed until Monday, April 18.
April 18, 1904	White students prevented entry of black students into the school. Superintendent Pearson closed school until fall of 1904.

April 23, 1904   Louis Gregory arraigned before Judge M. H. Donoho. Trial date set for June 6.

May 2, 1904   Citywide eighth-grade graduation exercises, traditionally held together, now separated to prevent mixing of the races.

June 6, 1904   Louis Gregory found guilty and sentenced to life in prison.

September 14, 1904   Segregation plan implemented on the basis of an unsigned memo. Sumner began as Manual Training High School. First black secondary teachers hired. J. E. Patterson appointed first principal and served to 1908.

January 25, 1905   Kansas City, Kansas School Board worked to present resolution providing for segregated schools to Kansas Legislature.

February 6, 1905   Kansas City, Kansas School Board passed resolution for the secondary school for black students—Manual Training High School.

1905–1908   Mr. J. E. Patterson appointed first principal and served for three years.

February 15, 1905   Citizens' group convened at Carnegie Library to discuss floating bonds to pay for building a separate school for blacks.

February 22, 1905   Kansas Legislature acted on resolution of the citizens' group and passed law that amended the General Statues of 1901. This marked the end of integrated education in Kansas.

February 28, 1905   General Statues were published to include segregation of schools. Manual training and instruction for the high school was specified in the new law.

May 1905   First class, comprised of six girls, graduated from Manual Training High School. Mytrle Jackson was the first class valedictorian.

June 1905   Manual Training School renamed Sumner High School.

June 6, 1905	KCK School Board bond election passed to build a separate school for blacks.
October 11, 1905	Legal challenge made to segregated schools by Mamie Richardson, a black student who attended Manual Training High School.
October 25, 1905	Kansas City, Kansas, School Board called meeting to discuss legal challenge by Mamie Richardson and delayed issuance of bonds.
June 25, 1906	Kansas Supreme Court ruled the segregated bill as constitutional.
	Mamie Richardson's challenge rendered null and void.
June 24, 1906	KCK Board of Education readied bonds for issuance to contractors.
Summer 1906	New high school built for black students over the summer.
September 1906	One hundred seventy-five students entered new building at Ninth Street and Washington Boulevard.
1908–1916	Mr. John Miller Marquess appointed and served as second principal.
September 1909	North wing added to the building.
1914	Sumner High School received coveted North Central Accreditation.
May 1916	John Hodge, chemistry teacher, was appointed principal of Sumner High School.
Fall 1919	The *Sumner Courier* was instituted.
November 1919	Night school began for community residents.
September 1923	Sumner implemented Normal Training Program for teacher certification.

September 1924	Sumner incorporated Junior College program. Mr. John Hodge appointed Assistant Dean of the Junior College Division.
1925	Gymnasium, cafeteria, and domestic science annex were built north of the main building.
October 28, 1932	Athletic field was dedicated.
1934	African American students in Johnson County, Edwardsville, and White Church areas began to be bused to Sumner High School.
May 1935	Students, under supervision of Scottie P. Davis, wrote the first history of Sumner High School. Student writers were from the class of 1935.
1938	Construction began on new Sumner building at Eighth and Oakland.
1940	New building was completed.
January 2, 1940	Classes began in the new building.
January 9, 1940	New building was dedicated.
May 1951 -	John Hodge retired as principal after thirty-five years of service.
1964	The field house of the athletic field was built.
1953–1972	S. H. Thompson began his administration.
1972–1973	Jerry Collier served as sixth ?principal.
1975	New gymnasium, cafeteria, and student center were added to the building.
1973–1978	James Boddie served as the last principal.
April 26, 1978	Students and faculty held tribute to school.
May 1978	Sumner High School closed its doors as a public high school.

KANSAS CITY, KANSAS HIGH SCHOOL

Sumner's existence has a complex and emotional origin. It evolved from a long-standing segregated school system that had been in place in elementary schools for over six decades. Black children were housed in substandard facilities and received poor fiscal support and inferior instructional resources in the segregated system. The black community decried these conditions on numerous occasions to the deaf ears of the Kansas City, Kansas School Board. Because of the opportunities and resources that would be available, blacks favored the integrated high school.[3] However, whites found a way to establish segregated schools.

From 1886 to 1904, Kansas City, Kansas High School was the only high school in the city. At that time, Kansas state law mandated segregation in the elementary schools but required local governments to establish integrated high schools.[4] Located on the northwest corner of Ninth Street and Minnesota Avenue, the Kansas City, Kansas High School constituted what eventually would become Wyandotte High School and the institution from which Sumner High School would evolve.[5]

Even though high schools throughout the state of Kansas were integrated, the climate all over the country was racially tense. During the early years of Kansas City, Kansas High School, less than 10 percent of the student population was nonwhite, and there were few overt racial problems. However, black students had difficult personal experiences resulting from the underlying tensions, which made their lives miserable at best. One such experience is that of Dora Evans, the first African-American student to receive her diploma from Kansas City, Kansas High School. She made the grade academically but suffered ridicule from her white peers, even until the day of graduation. She was selected to be one of the commencement speakers and addressed an important issue of the day. Her speech was titled, "Force of Revolution in the Face of the Race Problem." The *Wyandotte Gazette* reported that her remarks were timely and that she did a noble job. However, her presentation may have evoked her classmates' discomfort and anger. When she returned to her seat, students had moved, and there was noticeable confusion about where she

---

3 D. Lawrence, "The Impact of Local, State, and Federal Government Decisions on the Segregation and Subsequent Integration of Sumner High School in Kansas City, Kansas" (dissertation, 1998), 77–94.

4 W. W. Boone, "A History of Education in Kansas City, Kansas: Readin, Riting, Rithmetic." U.S.D. 500 (Kansas City, Kan.: Board of Education, 1986).

5 S. P. Davis, "The Story of Sumner High School" (Unpublished, 1935). Written by students, this is the first documented history of the school.

would sit. However, the matter was resolved when an unnamed white male offered to sit next to her. There is no doubt that there were similar stories etched in the hearts and diaries of black students who numbered about 75 in the 756-student body of 1903.

THE FATAL SHOT THAT BROUGHT DIVISION

The origins of Sumner High School are wedded to a fatal incident that occurred in a neighborhood park. On Tuesday, April 12, 1904, William Roy Martin, a Kansas City, Kansas High School student and member of a prominent white family, was killed suddenly and unpredictably. The story surrounding his death varies from its many iterations, but it was eventually accepted that during a baseball practice at Kerr Park, a confrontation arose between Roy and Louis Gregory, an eighteen-year-old black youth. Louis, who was not on the baseball team or even a student at the high school, was on a frog-hunting expedition with his friends in the park. He had a single-shot, .22-caliber gun in his possession. Louis and his companions had crossed the field, when an altercation erupted between the two groups. Within a matter of minutes, Roy Martin was dead, and Louis Gregory was detained and subsequently taken to the Wyandotte County Jail.

Stories of Roy's death spread like wildfire and set in motion a series of events that reversed the state law regarding public education and led to the segregation of Kansas City, Kansas High School. Mr. Orrin Murray, a local historian, provided an account that gave context and understanding to the rapid escalation of the incident. It is significant if not prophetic that black ministers had met earlier on the very day of the shooting. They had convened with Superintendent M. E. Pearson because of their concerns over the mounting tensions between the black and white communities. Mr. Pearson placated them by recommending that they provide counseling among their black citizenry.[6] Indeed, some form of mediation was needed before that very night ended.

By evening, those same black ministers were called into action. A group of approximately fifty black citizens, led by Reverend George McNeil and Reverend Thomas Knapper of Rose Hill Baptist Church (later to become Eighth Street Baptist Church), along with veterans of the Spanish-American War stood with rifles and shotguns. They were ready to guard the Wyandotte County Jail against

6 Lawrence (1998), p. 78.

a white mob that had formed with the intent of lynching Louis Gregory. As the mob approached, Reverend McNeil cocked his rifle and said there had been enough bloodshed that day. "Any man who crosses that curbstone will open his eyes in hell tomorrow." [7]

The day after the fatal incident and the gathering at the jail, black students reported to school as usual; however, they were confronted by approximately seven hundred white students, who barred them from entering. Many believed that the scene at the school was a result of the *Kansas City Star*'s false report of a race riot that allegedly took place the night before at the jail. It was erroneously and perhaps maliciously conveyed that a black mob descended on the jail to release Louis Gregory, and the incident ended in the arrest of six black youth. In truth, the black group had quelled the situation and prevented another lynching that was all too prevalent during those times, and there were no arrests. In response to the white students' uprising, Superintendent Pearson declared Kansas City, Kansas High School closed until the following Monday.

Research by Peavler pointed out that Martin's funeral service, held on Sunday, April 17, brought about a spirit of forgiveness and reconciliation, but it also revealed the ultimate intent of whites to separate the races.[8] Reverend Frank Fox of the First Congregational Church eulogized Martin by saying, "Separation of the races was the only solution ... the Negro is here to stay ... No human power can remove them from our midst. They are the nation's care and the white man's burden." [9] Reverend Fox's sentiments were later borne out in the manipulation of legislative, executive, and judicial branches of the state government to institute segregation in the public schools.

On April 18, the designated day when the school was to reopen, only a few students attempted to attend classes. But once again, white students blocked their black schoolmates from entering the building. The superintendent acted precipitously and closed the high school for the remainder of the school year.

On June 6, 1904, Louis Gregory was placed on trial for the murder of Roy Martin. Gregory, who was crippled, testified that he fired his gun to protect himself after Roy attacked him. Gregory's defense attorney pleaded that he should be

---

7 Lawrence (1998), p. 79.
8 D. J. Peavler, "Drawing the Color Line in Kansas City: The Story of Sumner High School." Kansas History: Journal of Central Plains 27 (Autumn 2005): 192–193.
9 Peavler (2005).

acquitted on the grounds of self-defense. The jury, however, found Gregory guilty and sentenced him to life in prison.[10]

SWIFT LEGISLATIVE ACTIONS TOWARD SEGREGATED HIGH SCHOOLS

Reactions to the critical incident that spawned the temporary closing of Kansas City, Kansas High School, and the ultimate segregation of all schools in the state, provided compelling evidence of the racial distrust and disrespect that permeated the times. In the wake of the tragic incident and as a result of the verdict, racial tensions continued to swell in the city. Talk of creating distinct schools for blacks and whites was fueled by local politics. Ambitious candidates who were running for state offices at the time used the opportunity to broker votes; they agreed to establish a segregated high school if that was what the public wanted. The killing in Kerr Park stirred up the entire community and marked the onset of a new day in public education in the state of Kansas.

Reactions developed into a series of racially divided meetings among white and black residents. Whites explored ways to ensure their children would not attend school with blacks, regardless of the state law that was in place. On the other hand, blacks focused on strategies to ensure their children would receive a quality education, and they knew that the needed resources would come only in an integrated environment. In large measure, both groups prevailed. Legal counsel representing the Kansas City, Kansas School Board drew up the following resolution, dated January 25, 1905, to summarize the occurrences of the previous year and to make recommendations for enacting a law to segregate the schools.

> Whereas, an unfortunate incident, having no bearing on the school system of Kansas City, Kansas, aroused the ire of a number of white patrons and white friends of the Kansas City, Kansas High School and caused them to use such an incident as a pretext to eject abruptly all colored students from said high school, to bar the doors against them, and to deny them privilege of attending said school, and whereas, said act is a gross violation of the school laws of the state of Kansas, and an infringement of the constitutional rights of the colored citizens of Kansas:
>
> Be it resolved that: (1) We condemn such an act as unconstitutional.

---

10 Davis (1935).

(2) We recommend that the colored students be restored their rights or that in the name of justice the school be closed to both races until such laws are enacted by the state legislature, repealing the law providing for Mixed high schools in Kansas City, Kansas, and enacting a law for separate high schools in Kansas City, Kansas.[11]

Whites moved forward with their plans to end integration, and blacks demanded that their children continue to attend the high school, despite the effort to block mixing of the races. A temporary compromise was agreed on until a final decision could be made at the scheduled meeting of the state legislature in February. Pending the outcome of the state meeting and prior to the opening of schools in fall of 1904, it was decided to house black and white students in the same building on a split schedule, since there were no facilities for separate high schools. White students attended school during the morning hours, 8:00 AM to 1:00 PM; black students attended in the afternoon, from 1:15 PM to 5:15 PM.

In September 1904, when the split schedule was implemented, the day school remained the Kansas City, Kansas High School; the afternoon school became known as Manual Training High School. This name was selected by the Kansas City, Kansas School Board but was highly protested by the black community because of the focus on manual labor. Kansas City, Kansas High School, now comprised of two separate schools, would later become Wyandotte High School and Sumner High School, respectively. Manual Training High School opened with a faculty of three new teachers and one administrator. It is noted that the Manual Training High School was the first setting in which black students were taught by black teachers at the high school level. The vanguards were Mr. G. F. Porter, Latin teacher; Ms. Florence Crews, English teacher; Mr. G. B. Buster, history teacher, and Mr. J. E. Patterson, principal. It was upon the shoulders of these four formidable leaders that a black high school of excellence was established. It continued to grow quantitatively and qualitatively for over seven decades.

At the January 1905 state legislative session, a bill, known as the "Segregated Bill," was passed and stamped as House Bill No. 890. The bill was specifically designed to govern the schools of Kansas City, Kansas, and to amend Section 6290 of the General Statutes of 1901. It reversed the provision for mixed high schools in the state of Kansas. Governor E. W. Hoch opposed the measure, maintaining that it was an injustice to penalize and further handicap an entire group for the actions

---

11 Davis (1935).

of one person. Notwithstanding, the Kansas City, Kansas, local government fully supported the school board's segregated policy and duplicitous actions.

Indeed, the bill did not pass without opposition. There was an individual student's petition as well as a group petition opposing the bill with 3,370 signatures. For a while, it even appeared that the bill would not meet the deadline and if so, would not pass. The passage came at the eleventh hour, because none of the Wyandotte County legislators wanted to introduce the bill. They wanted to deny the existence of racism, but the bill demonstrated their true feelings. Each legislator relied on the other to speak up. It was finally Representative Robinett who broke the ice.

The bill was passed; it was published in the official state paper, February 28, 1905. It was deemed the most "rushed legislation" ever passed in the state of Kansas at that time.[12] It was no ordinary beginning for an educational institution. These legislative actions are what set the Sumner High School story apart from the beginnings of other high schools of the era.

Prior to the bill's signing, the Kansas City, Kansas School Board had already been stealthily crafting and working to pass a resolution to build a segregated high school. Land had been identified at Ninth and Washington Boulevard and purchased. This was done without regard to legislative protocol. The strategic work to float a bond for a prematurely conceived segregated high school resulted in a swift public vote for a new building right after the passage of the Segregated Bill. Voters in all but one precinct were in favor of the bond to approve sixty thousand dollars to erect a new school. Forty thousand dollars was spent on the building itself, and twenty thousand dollars was set aside for equipment.

Mamie Richardson, an eighteen-year-old student who had attended the Manual Training High School, filed a lawsuit in the Kansas Supreme Court against the new segregation law on October 11, 1905. Her argument was based on the premise that the law violated the Constitution of the United States. She argued that her admittance to the Kansas City, Kansas High School should not be based on the color of her skin. Furthermore, she testified that the educational accommodations accorded African-American children in segregated schools were inferior, but the Supreme Court did not rule in her favor.

---

12 Boone (1986).

A NEW DAY, A NEW DIRECTION, A NEW SCHOOL

After the state law was passed, there was much unrest for the remainder of the year about the name, curricula and physical plant of the new school. Much of the debate of Sumner's future in preparing students focused on the two distinct educational philosophies of W. E. B. Du Bois and Booker T. Washington. Du Bois was deeply concerned with educating and developing the mind, while Washington advocated training the hands. Several open and closed meetings were held among prominent ministers, attorneys, teachers, and members of the Board of Education to address the concerns. The majority of parents and community leaders adamantly supported Du Bois's philosophy. They felt it would provide the foundation for a classical curriculum, which would prepare students for a broad range of professional career choices. It was in the home of Dr. Corrvine Patterson that the instructional focus was finally decided. In June 1905, it was also settled that the imposed name of Manual Training High School would have to be dropped.

It is significant to note that prior to the agreement, and in protest to a focus on "manual training," a number of black parents pulled their children out of the afternoon high school and enrolled them in Western University (a Civil War Freedmen's Bureau school established in the Quindaro area of Kansas City, Kansas). Western University enrolled black adolescents and young adults from around the country as well as the local area. The school fostered a comprehensive curriculum that offered both classical and vocational training.

During the summer of 1905, the new school building was erected at Ninth Street and Washington Boulevard, next to Douglass Elementary School. Although the new building needed minor carpentry for completion, 178 students entered in September 1905, eager and ready to learn. Since the designation Manual Training School had been dropped, the new school building was opened without a name. Four additional faculty members were assigned: Mr. J. P. King, biological science teacher; Ms. Beulah Burke, domestic arts teacher; Ms. Minnie Howell, English teacher; and Mr. George H. Mowbray, manual training instructor.

SUMNER, A NAME OF DISTINCTION

There are lots of considerations that go into the naming of a new educational institution. But with Sumner's establishment, it was immediately realized that coming to consensus on a name had the ability to unify the Kansas City, Kansas,

African-American community. Whereas the elementary schools increased contacts among parents of particular neighborhoods, Sumner brought together black families from all parts of the city and created an educational community for its black youth. In June 1905, as the construction of the new high school was under way, Superintendent Pearson and Sumner faculty members worked together in the Board of Education office of the Carnegie Library to decide on a name that would bring honor to the school. There was great deliberation over names of leaders who exemplified high principles and values, distinguished themselves as leaders, and who had rendered great service to our nation. Men such as Abraham Lincoln, Frederick Douglass, Booker T. Washington, and Charles Sumner were discussed. Two of these favored names had already been given to schools within the area. There was Douglass Elementary in Kansas City, Kansas, and Lincoln High School in the sister city of Kansas City, Missouri. Washington was not selected because Booker T. Washington was still living. In addition, many of the black citizens did not agree with Washington's philosophy and expressed strong sentiments against his advocacy of vocational training for their children.

The name Sumner was finally selected in honor of abolitionist and statesman Charles Sumner. Sumner was venerated for his endless efforts to achieve equality for blacks in all walks of life. His exceptional scholarship goals and ideals were deeply rooted in high morals and Christian beliefs. Unlike the majority of his white counterparts, who ultimately came to prominence in American life, Sumner was born of great lineage and wealth. His family was part of the old New England aristocracy. The Sumner family was known for its intellectual acuity, cultural awareness, and civic and social sense of responsibility. Charles Sumner had inherited all of these dynamic leadership attributes and fought vigorously for the rights of African Americans.

Sumner was born in Boston and attended Boston Latin School. He attended Harvard, as did his father, and graduated in 1830. He was admitted to the Boston Bar Association in 1834, and was offered a professorship at Harvard but declined it. Sumner's life's work began in Massachusetts, where he tried to extend public education to all of its residents. In 1849, he argued before the Massachusetts Supreme Court against the expulsion of the daughter of a black printer in Boston from a nearby public school because of her color. Although he lost the case, his arguments cleared the way for the 1855 Massachusetts law that outlawed segregation in public schools.

Sumner succeeded Daniel Webster in the U.S. Senate in 1851. He began almost immediately to fight for emancipation. His first great antislavery speech, Freedom National, in August 1852 denounced the Fugitive Slave Act. Sumner continued to speak out against slavery and the Southern "slave power," as he called it, throughout the 1850s. It is said that his "Crime against Kansas" speech in 1856 (several days before John Brown's raid at Pottawatomie Creek in Kansas City, Kansas) was delivered with such fervor that he angered South Carolina Congressman Preston Brooks, who physically attacked him with a cane on the Senate floor. Sumner was injured so severely that he was not able to appear in public for three years after the attack.

Literally to his dying day, Charles Sumner worked to obtain civil rights for black citizens. No doubt he had great satisfaction in his role of issuing the Emancipation Proclamation in January 1863. One of his greatest victories was witnessing the passage of the Thirteenth and Fourteenth Amendments, which gave African Americans full citizenship.

It was the vision and hope of the new Sumner High School faculty that every boy and girl who passed through the halls of the new school would learn to emulate the courage, broadmindedness, virtues, and character of the man whose name the school bore. They believed this name gave black citizens a greater sense of pride and optimism for the future than the name Manual Training High School could have ever evoked.

SUMNER'S GROWTH AND EVOLUTION TOWARD ACADEMIC EXCELLENCE

During the first twenty-five years of the new century, Sumner High School grew slowly but steadily. Once the new building was completed, black parents eagerly sent their children to the high school. Within a year's time, classes had grown so large that it was necessary to add a north wing at a cost of twenty thousand dollars.

Sumner's first principal, Mr. J. E. Patterson, provided direction and leadership to Sumner's faculty and student body until 1908. The staff worked diligently to develop the school into a college-preparatory high school equal to the Kansas City, Kansas High School. As new faculty members were added to the staff, they not only sought to educate the students but made every effort to become involved in the community. In 1908, Principal John Miller Marquess took over the leadership and spearheaded the expansion of student enrollment and instructional programs. During the 1908–1909 school year, the north wing of the school was added to the main building.[13] By 1914, the student body had grown to 220, with ten new faculty members. To better serve the community, Principal Marquess instituted an evening adult education program, which mirrored night classes at the Kansas City, Kansas High School. On Mr. Marquess's departure to head Western University in 1916, Mr. Garfield A. Curry, teacher, provided leadership to develop further the night school program.

By 1920, Mr. Curry had instituted classes in commercial music, sewing, millinery arts, auto mechanics, cabinetmaking, tailoring, and cooking in response to the community's needs. Enrollment in these courses exceeded the school's capacity. Thus, Douglass, Stowe, and Bruce elementary Elementary Schools and Argentine High School were established as satellite evening sites.

The Board of Education required every student enrolled in the evening school to pay a one dollar deposit, which was refundable if the student attended at least 75 percent of the class sessions. Whether this was intended as an incentive or deterrent is questionable. But Mr. Curry's convictions made the advantages of the offerings quite clear, "Night School stood for the abolishment of illiteracy among Negroes. Remember this, and also bear in mind that without education and culture, no race of people has risen to supremacy."[14]

At the end of Mr. Marquess' administration, the school experienced transformational leadership in the life and administration of Mr. John Hodge, former chemistry teacher. Excerpts from an article of the *Sumner Courier* dated October 17, 1921, summarize the growth in enrollment.

Sumner High School Gains 100 in Two Years

Sumner High School started off with the pistol shot on September 12, with 401 in their seats. The pupils had been enrolled the week before so that no time would be lost… One stepping in to visit that day would have thought school had been going on for at least a week. The periods were run on schedule. The lunch room was ready for service …

---

13 Boone (1986).

14 Sumner Courier (October 15, 1923). 1 (1). Curry's philosophy on literacy in the community is used to encourage enrollment.

Principal J. A. Hodge was greatly surprised to find so many enrolling for the Freshman Class … It was his opinion that Kansas City, Kansas had ceased to receive people from other states lying immediately to the south but this is not true. People are still flocking northward, as shown by the information cards pupils are required to fill out. Oklahoma, Arkansas, and Texas are states sending the largest numbers.

Programs also flourished. In 1923, under Mr. Hodge's helm, Sumner adopted college curricula. A training program for selected high school seniors who wanted to go into the teaching profession was established, and junior college was instituted for those who had already graduated. The normal school course of study (teacher preparation) resulted in a significant number of Sumner graduates becoming classroom teachers in the segregated schools of Kansas City, Kansas. The institution of junior college was another effort to ensure that residents reaped the full benefits of education. Curriculum requirements were the same as those of Kansas City, Kansas Junior College. Courses that were successfully completed at Sumner were fully transferable to other state colleges in Kansas, including Kansas University and Kansas State Agricultural College at Manhattan. There was no tuition; residents who had completed four years of high school qualified to enroll in the collegiate program which continued until 1951.[15]

The first teachers in the junior college were: Ms. Scottie P. Davis, English; Mr. Earl A. Taylor, English and history; and Mr. H. S. Williams, chemistry. Mr. Hodge was appointed the assistant dean of the Sumner Junior College Division.

In light of the growth in student enrollment and the expansion of programs, the physical plant of Sumner High School was destined to expand. During the years 1924-1930, the auditorium was made into four classrooms. During the Depression years, when the number of graduates continued to grow, the Board of Education was convinced of the need to purchase land for a new building. The site would not only house a new building, but an athletic field was also promised. This decision came in 1932, but an unfortunate (some say more suspicious than unfortunate) incident delayed the land purchase and construction of the new building. Abruptly on March 3, 1934, disaster came to Wyandotte High, formerly known as Kansas City, Kansas High School. A fire destroyed the school, and immediate plans for replacement of the white high school took priority over the building preparations for Sumner.

15 Sumner Courier (November 15, 1923): 1 (1, 2)l.

41

It was not until 1938 that the board declared the absolute inadequacy of the old Sumner building and found it necessary to build a new school. While $2.5 million was spent on replacing Wyandotte just four years earlier, only $751,000 was authorized for constructing Sumner. The building was designed to house the following complement of rooms: fourteen general classrooms, two music rooms, one drama and speech room, four home economics rooms, one health and beauty culture room, one drawing and art room, six shop classes, six life science rooms, six physical science classes, an eighty-eight-student capacity library, and an auditorium for one thousand five hundred occupants. Since Sumner also served as a junior college, rooms were provided for those collegiate classes as well. Moving day from the old building to the new building was December 15, 1939.

During his thirty-five years as principal, Mr. John Hodge played a major role in the lives of the students as well as the Kansas City, Kansas community. He believed in the capability of all black youth. He did not want them to think of themselves as inadequate, and he did everything in his power to see to it that his students were successful. He was regarded as one of the most brilliant educators of his time.[16] At his retirement celebration, the superintendent of Kansas City, Kansas schools acknowledged Mr. Hodge as an, "outstanding administrator, having developed Sumner High School from a small high school to its present outstanding position—one which is recognized all over the nation."[17]

Mr. Solomon H. Thompson, Jr. succeeded Mr. Hodge and continued the high standards that had made Sumner a beacon on the hill. He is recognized for keeping the school on a high academic track and for implementing strong disciplinary procedures. Mr. Thompson served the community and Sumner for twenty-one years.

RESTRUCTURING SCHOOLS

In an information-gathering session of the Sumner Alumni Association held in July of 2006, alumni expressed sentiments that the Sumner story could not be told in its entirety without acknowledging the education Sumnerians received at Northeast Junior High School. Northeast did play a significant role, but so did the elementary schools whose histories are intertwined in the history of Northeast.

---

16 Boone (1986).
17 Lawrence (1998).

The elementary schools that fed into Northeast and Sumner were Attucks, Bruce, Douglass, Dunbar North, Dunbar South, Grant, Kealing, Lewis, Lincoln, Stowe, Vernon, and Washington.[18] Of this group of feeder schools, only Douglass and Grant Elementary Schools served the community at the date of this publication.

Because of segregation, Northeast Junior High School and Sumner High School served as magnets for black students in the area and those outside the Kansas City, Kansas School District boundaries. The outside areas included Argentine, Armourdale, Armstrong, Edwardsville, Greystone Heights, Quindaro, Rosedale, Shawnee Mission, West Bottoms, and White Church.

To maintain the segregated system, the Kansas City, Kansas School District paid the fare for "out of walking distance" students for more than twenty-five years. Two bus companies, McCallop and Rucker, were contracted to transport these students to and from school for over twenty-five years. The district also provided streetcar tokens for "long-distance" students attending Northeast and Sumner. With black students coming from multiple neighborhoods to a limited number of black schools, overcrowding was an issue. Because of the value the community placed on education, students learned to endure the long rides and the crowded classrooms.

Even though Northeast was organized in 1923 as the second junior high school in the city, classes were not held in the building until 1925. Prior to its existence, students attended the black elementary schools until the completion of their eighth-grade year. Northeast was built on historic grounds previously owned by the Wyandot Indian tribe and later by the Fowler family, owner of the Fowler Meat Packing Company of Kansas City, Missouri. It was located at Fourth and Troup, overlooking Rattlebone Hollow, in the largest black district of Kansas City, Kansas.

Northeast Junior High School was organized to facilitate a more comprehensive education for young adolescents and to alleviate the problems of overcrowding at Sumner High School. It was also designed to perpetuate a segregated system that had been instituted in the Kansas City, Kansas School District. Just as Sumner benefited from a racist society that closed professional opportunities to blacks, resulting in top black scholars becoming teachers, so did Northeast and the feeder elementary schools.

---

18 Lawrence (1998), pp. 111–112.

The first principal of Northeast was Mr. J. P. King. In keeping with his insistence on excellence, the school motto became "Be the Best." Mr. King opened the building at Fourth and Troup with 525 students, and eighteen faculty members. He served as principal from 1923 until 1930, when he moved on to become the president of Western University.

Mr. Joseph H. Collins, a 1915 graduate of Sumner High School, was the second principal of Northeast. He continued Mr. King's mantra of "Be the Best" for twenty-nine dedicated years. A powerful demonstration of his recognition of the best is evidenced in one of the visits he facilitated to the school by the renowned naturalist/scientist George Washington Carver. Exposure of students to possibilities for themselves was part and parcel of his charge. Principal Collins voiced his belief that junior high life was a time filled with transitions. He was convinced that the need for emphasizing respect for self and others, personal growth, and maturity were critical tasks of junior high school. His convictions were apparent in the opportunities he orchestrated for students and captured succinctly in one of his commencement speeches:

World changes and different living conditions during modern times have imposed new functions upon the junior high school. One of these is the need for each boy and girl early in life to understand himself; to understand the dignity and worth of every other human being on the face of the earth. In other words, each pupil is to begin early in life to evolve a sense of human dignity. Another is the duty to aid each student during his junior high school career to gain the self-confidence, the poise necessary to meet the perplexities of his daily living.

During his tenure from 1930 to 1958, Mr. Collins was not only noted for his support of the junior high school concept, but also for his sternness and strict discipline policies.

Mr. William Boone took the helm in the fall of 1958. His emphases were on academics, increasing teacher involvement in curricular decisions, and improving the quality of teacher preparation. He attempted to intensify the meaning of "Be the Best" for all students by instituting a number of changes. Under his leadership, a charter of the National Honor Society was established; it was the first such membership for a junior high school in the area. Future Teachers of America and a program to support pregnant teens in continuing their education were also instituted. Student participation in extracurricular activities, including sports, also increased under Mr. Boone's leadership from 1958 to 1973.

Two other principals served as the head of Northeast Junior High School: Mr. Arnold Webb, 1973–1975 and Mr. William C. Walker, 1975–1977.

Without argument, Northeast Junior High School was very important; it prepared students for meeting the demands of senior high school. It was a critical learning ground for transitioning from Dragons to Spartans (from fire-spitting animals to strategic, victorious humans). It was a critical precursor to good ole Sumner High.

In 1977, the U.S. District Court for the State of Kansas ruled that the school district had based its boundaries and location of Northeast Junior High on segregation laws, and this was not legal, nor constitutional. For half a century, Northeast Junior High School prepared all who entered her walls to achieve excellence by being the best. Northeast was closed in 1977.

Figure 3.1 Old Sumner Building (1906)

Figure 3.2   Gymnasium (added to building in 1925)

Figure 3.3   Mr. John A. Hodge,
Principal (1908 – 1951)

Figure 3.4   Mr. John J. Lewis,
Vice Principal (1911- unknown)

Figure 3.5   1919 Faculty Portrait

Figure 3.6   Senior Class of 1919

Figure 3.7   Graduating Class of 1921

Figure 3.8   Early Girls Gym class (after 1925)

Figure 3.9 Early Boys Gym class (after 1925)

CHAPTER FOUR

WHAT KEPT SUMNER TOGETHER

It [Sumner] was a veritable blessing in disguise—a flower of which we may proudly say, "The bud had a bitter taste, but sweet indeed is the flower."

— Scottie P. Davis, 1935

Required by a 1905 state law, Sumner's creation in and of itself could not have ensured that the institution would become distinguished as an outstanding center of learning. In fact, the odds were against such an outcome. After all, the impetus for establishing this school was the elimination of further violence following the tragic death of a white youth involved in a confrontation with a black youth. There were no noble concerns or interests in elevating the educational level of blacks by the majority community, who were suddenly demanding separate schools at the secondary level. Moreover, black school administrators, teachers, and the black community at-large had no experience in structuring and running a high school. The question emerges, how was it possible for a group of black leaders, entering unchartered waters, to develop and sustain a reputable institution of learning?

There are various ways this question might be answered. By looking at intangible factors, the many aspects of caring and sacrifice provided by teachers and administrators begin to surface. Additionally, the sense of togetherness felt by students becomes evident, and the pride engendered by the beauty of the physical facility is understood. These are all valid factors that contribute to Sumner's viability, which endured for seven decades. This section, while recognizing the value of such intangible factors, chronicles the more tangible elements that not only were articulated by alumni but were referenced in research material, such as available published literature and archived documents. Thus, four distinct areas have been identified as critically impacting the school's prolonged success. They are the faculty, curricula, co-curricular programs, and the evidence of high standards and expectations.

FACULTY

John Hodge didn't play!! Apparently he had a "free" hand under school superintendent F. L. Schlagle [superintendent from 1932 to 1962] … The teachers were class acts; they spoke openly about "preparing" us.

— Donald E. Jackson, Class of 1944

Faculty prepared me not only for college but for life. I felt morally and socially prepared as a mature adult.

— Carolyn Mitchell, Class of 1965

As noted by Donna Foote, the quality of the teacher is the most important factor impacting student achievement.[19] The permanent imprint made by administrators and teachers on the lives of thousands of students over Sumner's existence cannot be overstated. The original school was established in a hurried fashion, within seventeen months after the mandate for a segregated high school. There were eighty students and four faculty members in the inaugural Sumner class of 1906. The faculty included the principal, J. E. Patterson; Mr. G. F. Porter, Latin teacher; Ms. Florence Crews, English teacher; and Mr. G. B. Buster, history teacher. Though few in number, the faculty worked hard and were committed to providing a first-class education. It is important to emphasize that the initial faculty's abiding belief in the value of advanced education was not mere rhetoric; it was clearly reflected in the number and level of their own degrees during a time when few blacks could boast of having finished high school, let alone college.

Mr. Greene B. Buster held both a bachelor's degree and a master's degree in education from Kansas University. Not only was Mr. Buster a teacher, he was also a prolific writer, who penned a textbook for a history of England course taught at the junior college. A novel written by Buster, *Brighter Sun,* received international as well as national acclaim, winning the Pageant Press Best-Book Award in 1954. The following excerpts from reviews of his work capture its essence and acclaim.

Written with simple sincerity and tremendous power, BRIGHTER SUN is the eloquent story of a man's struggle for freedom, and is particularly concerned with the American Negro. Objective and factual, it re-enacts the

---

19 D. Foote, Resentless Pursuit: A Year in the Trenches with Teach for America. (New York:Random House Publishers, 2009).

way of life that ended with the American Civil War. Its scenes are vivid, and its emotions authentically genuine. (*The Book Exchange, Sardinia House, Kingsway, London, England*)

No book dealing with slavery touches the heart strings more forcibly than does Greene B. Buster's BRIGHTER SUN, which gives a vivid picture of the struggles of his grandfather, Garret Buster, to free himself and his family from the bonds of slavery. (*Pittsburgh Courier*, Pittsburgh, Pennsylvania)

Figure 4.1 Mr. G. B. Buster, Constitution and American History Teacher

Between 1900 and 1909, 1,613 black men and women earned college degrees, which added to the aggregate 2,500 degrees earned in prior years. By 1936, some 44,000 college and professional degrees had been conferred on blacks who numbered 12.5 million, nationwide. Statistically, in 1936, this represented .35 percent of the black population that had four or more years of college. "Those who did have college degrees enjoyed special distinction and were expected to assume leadership roles."[20]

---

20 W. B. Gatewood, Aristocrats of Color. The Black Elite 1880–1920. (Bloomington: Indiana University Press, 1990).

Holding together the faculty was an extraordinary set of principals, four of them rendering service over a span of sixty-seven years. These distinguished men were Mr. J. E. Patterson (1905–1908), Mr. John Marquess (1908–1916), Mr. John A. Hodge (1916–1951), and Mr. Solomon H. Thompson Jr. (1951–1972). In 1916, Mr. Marquess resigned to accept the presidency of Langston University in Langston, Oklahoma. Mr. Hodge, a trained chemist, was a member of Sigma Xi, an honorary scientific society. He had published in a 1910 edition of "School Science and Mathematics," an article on the electric arc. Prior to his taking over the reins, Mr. Thompson served as a representative on the Kansas City, Kansas Planning Commission and was supervisor of African-American elementary schools in the city. Each succeeding principal upheld the standards that had been set in place and passed on as a part of the school's legacy. Prior to the transition to Sumner Academy, the last principals who served were Jerry Collier (1972–1973) and James Boddie (1973–1978).

Along with the student body, the Sumner faculty increased steadily over the decades. But in keeping with the high value placed on education, the credentials of faculty did not lessen. Figures 4.2 and 4.3 are rosters from the school years 1926–1927 and 1934–1935, which show faculty degrees and the institutions from which they were earned.

Figure 4.2 Faculty Roster 1926 – 1927 (41 percent held a master's degree in 1927)

Andrews, Grace M. (English/Journalism) A.B. University of Denver
Buster, G. B. (Constitution, American History) B.S. Kansas University, Wilberforce University
Branch, Mary E. (English, Psychology) A.B. and A. M. University of Chicago
Curry, G. A. (Latin) A.B., M.A. University of Chicago
Davis, Scottie P. (English) A.B. University of Minnesota
Hodge, John A. (Psychology) A.B., A.M. University of Indiana
Jackson, Vera (French, Mathematics) A.B. University of Kansas
Lewis, J.J. (Mathematics, Discipline Hall) A. B. New Orleans University
McNorton, Florence (Domestic Science) B.S. Howard University
Mowbray, G. H. (Manual Arts) A.B. Howard University
Murry, F. Luther (English, constitution) A.B. Lincoln University; A.M. Columbia
Pendleton, Emma A. (Commercial Branches) Drake Business College, New York
Penman, Beatrice E. (Physical Training, English) B.S. Ohio State University
Reynolds, T. H. (Music) A.B. Indiana University; Oberlin Conservatory of Music
Smith, Ruth B. (French, English) A.B. Wittenberg College
Taylor, E.A. (Biology, Botany) B.A. Wilberforce; A.M. Columbia
Williams, H. S. (Physics, Chemistry) A.B. Oberlin College; A.M University of Chicago
Wright, Edwina (Domestic Art) A.B. University of Pennsylvania; A.M. Columbia University

Figure 4.3 Faculty Roster 1934 – 1935 (61 percent held a master's degree in 1935)

Anderson, L.A. (Foods) B.S. Kansas State Teachers College at Pittsburg;
University of Chicago

Buster, G. B. (History, Civics), B.A., M.S. University of Kansas

Curry, G.A. (History) B.A. Morehouse; M.A. University of Chicago;
University of Kansas; University of Colorado

Davis, Scottie P. (English) A.B. University of Minnesota; Ed.M. Harvard
University; Columbia University

Hodge, John A. (Principal) B.A., M.A. University of Indiana; M.A.;
University of Chicago, University of Wisconsin, University of Kansas,
University of Colorado

Mowbray, G. H. (Industrial Arts) A.B. Howard University; Teachers College,
Chicago University, Kansas State Teachers College at Emporia;
Iowa State University

Hoffman, E.N. (English) B.A. Howard University; M.A. Columbia University

McKee, D.K. (Home Economics) B.S. Kansas State Teachers College at
Pittsburg; University of Colorado; University of Chicago

Reynolds, T.H. (Music) B.A. University of Indiana; Oberlin University,
University of Kansas

Spears, M.C. (Commercial Studies) B.A. University of Southern California;
M.A. University of Kansas

Thatcher, J. L. (U.S. Constitution) B.A. Hampton Institute; University of
Kansas; University of Minnesota

Thornton, H.B. (Mathematics) B.A. Howard University; M.A. University of
Cincinnati; University of Chicago

Wynbush, O.B. (English) B.A. Oberlin University; M.A. Columbia University

By 1930, student enrollment warranted a faculty of eighteen, 44 percent of whom had earned master's degrees, as noted in an article appearing in the *Kansas City Star,* November 2, 1996. By understanding the proportion of all U.S. citizens who earned college degrees during this period, one gains a better appreciation of the accomplishments of Sumner's teachers. Figure 4.4 provides this insight. By 1935, the number of teachers holding a master's degree jumped to approximately 61 percent, notably among the most highly trained high school professionals in the state. There is no doubt that employment opportunities outside the black community were nearly nonexistent due to both segregation and widespread racial discrimination. Thus, these practices accounted for the high concentration of exceptionally well-educated teachers who found their way to and remain at the school for decades. It was not uncommon for individual teachers to remain at Sumner for thirty years or more. These capable, long-term instructors were given a great deal of respect and admiration from successive generations of community residents and students. A significant number of the early faculty became legendary. Such names and personalities etched in alumni's memories include those listed in the chart titled Some Amazing Teachers, Figure 4.5.

Figure 4.4   Percent of the Population 25 years and over with a Bachelor's Degree or More

Digest of Education Statistics, published by the
National Center for Education Statistics, 2001.

1910	....	2.7%	March 1988 ..	20.3%
1920	....	3.3%	March 1989 ..	21.1%
1930	....	3.9%	March 1990 ..	21.3%
April 1940	......	4.6%	March 1991 ..	21.4%
April 1950	.....	6.2%	March 1992 ..	21.4%
April 1960	....	7.7%	March 1993 ..	21.9%
March 1970 ..		11.0%	March 1994 ..	22.2%
March 1975 ..		13.9%	March 1995 ..	23.0%
March 1980 ..		17.0%	March 1996 ..	23.6%
March 1982 ..		17.7%	March 1997 ..	23.9%
March 1985 ..		19.4%	March 1998 ..	24.4%
March 1986 ..		19.4%	March 1999 ..	25.2%
March 1987 ..		19.9%	March 2000 ..	25.6%

Figure 4.5 Some Amazing Teachers that Spanned the Years

Aulette Abernathy	English
Winifred D. Anderson	Cosmetology
Eugene Banks	American History
Edward Beasley	American History
Rebecca Bloodworth	English
William Boone	Chemistry
James A. Bradford	Machine Shop
G. B. Buster	History
Tallulah Carey	Mathematics
E. A. Charlton	Journalism
Robert Clark	Instrumental Music
Garfield Curry	Latin
Rosemary Daniels	Cosmetology
Scottie P. Davis	English, Physical Training
A. T. Edwards	Industrial Arts
George Green	Mathematics
Gerald Hall	History
John Henderson	Industrial Arts
Kenneth Hill	Physical Education
Edna Hoffman	English
Vera Jackson	French I, Algebra I
Roberta Jeltz	Nurse
R. Rostel Mansfield	Algebra, Mathematics
Percy H. McDavid	Music
Dimple McGee	English
Paul L. Mobiley	Chemistry
Delores Moore	Foods
George Mowbray	Industrial Arts
Beatrice Penman	English – Counselor
T. H. Reynolds	Music
Christine Sears	Librarian
William Smith	Physics, Mathematics
Mack Spears	Typewriting
Grace Stevens	Home Economics
Oyarma Tate	Vocal Music
Earl A. Taylor	Biology
Charles Terry	Industrial Arts
James Thatcher	U. S. Government
Harry Thornton	Mathematics
Clarence Turpin	Mathematics

Even in comparison with teaching standards of today, the level of academic achievement earned by early faculties is impressive. It should be kept in mind that from 1905 through the 1950s, there were significantly greater obstacles for blacks to overcome in their quest for a college degree. There were no Pell grants or student loan programs, college deans and professors freely used discriminatory practices to assess achievement of blacks or to prevent them from entering college, and career options after graduation were very limited. As for the group of educators who found their way to Sumner, many of them attended multiple colleges and universities in diverse cities to gain their degree(s), a feat reflective of their perseverance and determination. (Refer to figures 4.2 and 4.3.)

Later in life, I realized what a great sacrifice our black teachers made for us and how much love and concern they had—desiring to bring the best out of us. I am grateful for their sacrifices.

— Johnnie Mae McGentry-Crane, Class of 1930

The teachers and the setting were "class acts." They spoke openly about "preparing us."

— Donald E. Jackson, Class of 1944

Our teachers were well prepared educators, which gave all of us a feeling of security and satisfaction.

— Albertine Everett Morgan, Class of 1948

During my extensive academic endeavors, my Sumner teachers were second to none.

— Richard M. Hopkins, Class of 1952

I got through Ms. Bloodworth's class with 4s. I took the English admittance exam and had the second-highest score at Langston University. Ms. Bloodworth told me, "I knew you had it all the time."

— John Yates, Class of 1956

Then it happened! One day in Ms. Bloodworth's class we were given a sentence to diagram on the blackboard. Our task was to designate the parts of speech.

After a few minutes, one word was not correctly placed. Ms. Bloodworth began to sincerely cry. She said, "I cannot believe that you young people did not know where the one word, which is a gerund, did not belong. There is so much work to be done to prepare you for college."

— George Crump, Class of 1962

By the end of the 1960s, after passage of the Civil Rights Bill, the faculty of Sumner had become more diversified and, some would argue, less highly qualified. With a faculty of forty-eight full-time members in 1968, only 35 percent held a master's degree. In the 1974–1975 "Self Study Report" for the North Central Association of Colleges and Secondary Schools and Kansas State Department of Education, it is significant to note what the Evaluation Committee stated about its staff, "Excellence of education is being achieved through an adequately trained staff." In the early years of Sumner, there was no argument: the staff was highly trained in their respective fields. The term "adequate" would never have been used to describe their preparation. Throughout the first six decades of Sumner, alumni have been quick and accurate in giving tribute to the academic excellence of their teachers in both public and private forums. Unusual even for the twentieth century, students from the Class of 1919 wrote a general chronology of their three-year experience at Sumner as a tribute to their teachers. "Appreciation to Our Teachers" written by Cecial F. T. Carroll, was published in their yearbook and recognizes some of the early teachers across subject areas.

Appreciation to Our Teachers

Mr. Curry was our most amusing teacher, although we found nothing amusing in our Latin nor in the 3's and 4's he gave us. We constantly heard this remark from Mr. Curry when one of our popular gentleman classmates would doze off for a quiet sleep: "Now, Anderson, since you don't have any lesson, you could stay awake and try to absorb some knowledge." Or he would say to a nearby classmate, "Go get some water and put on that fellow," or "Man, they are going to arrest you." Through all this we learned Latin and appreciated Mr. Curry's care and patience; for we are sure it took a great deal of patience to deal with such an "ignorant bunch" of Freshmen.

The girls spent many enjoyable hours under their patient and quiet teacher, Miss Katie Davis. The girls, when mixing up a certain food, were inclined to take a little more to eat. Usually the girls would take too much butter, but before we left we had heard this statement, "You girls are going heavy on butter," so often that it impressed deeply on our minds, and most of the parents give Miss Davis credit for the girls using and eating less butter now than ever before.

Many and varied were the experiences we had under Miss Scottie Davis, our main English teacher. Though Miss Davis thought us an intolerable set of "Hottentots," she certainly made us learn English. We, too, appreciate her efforts, for they were strenuous ones. I am sure that before we left her control we were no longer "Fijis" but really civilized Sophomores, ready for Sophomore English.

Of Miss Burke we all know, for she in her very quiet and agreeable manner, taught us the principles of sewing. We are indeed grateful to her for her extreme kindness and wish to assure her that she will never be forgotten.

The boys experienced Mr. Mowbray's teaching in manual training and mechanical drawing. His training was careful and interesting and many of the boys completed the year successfully, saying they never saw such a "little man" know so much.

The majority of our classmates were successful in passing this year's work, which was very hard to do, since we were compelled to get accustomed to High School, together with its teachers. Those fortunate ones were well prepared to enter the Sophomore year.

Our Sophomore year was spent with these same teachers, with few exceptions. Mr. Curry was as amusing as ever. We had considered ourselves civilized, but Miss Davis still considered us "Fijis." Of course our lessons were harder, but our teachers made greater efforts than before and by the hardest work we pulled through to our Junior year. We had begun to think of examination, and many of us began to do a little more work.

Our Junior year brought some new teachers, Mr. King and Miss Pendleton. Mr. Curry, as usual, had us in Cicero.

We cannot even express our great appreciation of Mr. King for his kindness and instruction, for he is one of the most interesting, instructive and patient teachers we have ever had.

We are also grateful to Miss Pendleton, though at times some of us were very much discouraged to climb that long flight of steps to receive our six weeks grade of a 6. We see now that it was for our own good.

With these new teachers and the old ones we passed to the last or Senior year, but it meant by no means less work.

During our Senior year we met Mr. Buster in American History and Mr. Williams in Chemistry. In Mr. Buster's class the effort was all on the students' part, for it was with great effort that we could come up to the standards which Mr. Buster required.

Mr. Williams, our chemistry teacher, deserves much credit and appreciation for his careful teaching. We feel that we know a little chemistry, anyhow.

Our teachers have all been very kind, careful and considerate, and we sincerely appreciated their efforts, which we know were numerous. Every teacher may be assured that, though we shall not be with them another year, we shall ever cherish the memory of the many happy days we spent with them at Sumner High School.

CURRICULA

The segregated public school systems of Kansas City, Kansas, and Kansas City, Missouri, seemed to offer a quality education, but they were a far cry from being "equal" to the schools white students attended. Consider, for example, that Wyandotte High School in Kansas City, Kansas, that whites attended offered courses in German, Italian, Russian, Spanish, French, Latin, and Chinese, whereas Sumner High School that blacks attended only offered Spanish, French, and Latin. Wyandotte also offered swimming, golf, tennis, archery, softball, baseball, football, and basketball and fielded teams in those sports. Sumner, on the other hand, only offered swimming, football, and basketball. Wyandotte had two gymnasiums and two swimming pools; Sumner had one gym and one swimming pool. The comparison clearly reveals that the course offerings and the facilities were separate but not equal. Notwithstanding these inequities, the segregated schools were an important part of our community.

— Elmer Jackson III, Class of 1958

After being in existence for less than a decade, the vision and efforts of the faculty merited Sumner full accreditation by the Kansas North Central Association of Secondary Schools and Colleges.[21] This distinction was important, because the association was responsible for monitoring, evaluating, and reporting on the ability of high schools within its jurisdiction to implement basic curricula required by the State Board of Education. In-depth analyses of course offerings were done about every ten years, and findings were reported to the Board of Education and the superintendent of schools. These reports were the basis for determining whether schools would receive accreditation—whether they met nationally and internationally recognized academic standards. Applications from students graduating from an accredited institution were looked at more favorably by colleges and universities throughout the nation.

From the inception of Sumner, black educators had uppermost in mind the welfare of students and their futures. Consequently, they protested against the Kansas Board of Education (BOE) and insisted that a college-preparatory education be the school's major focus; the BOE wanted the school to specialize in vocational and manual training. Though the BOE failed in determining the school's major focus, it successfully required some manual training courses to be taught. No such requirement existed at the two other high schools—Kansas City, Kansas High School and Argentine High. Due to the inherent applications of vocational training in the workplace, this training proved profitable for many Spartans. In light of the relatively low number of students who had the financial means to attend college, this was especially true. To complete requirements for high school graduation, students had to earn eighteen credits, with boys taking at least three courses in shop work, that is, bench, lathes, or auto. Girls were required to take three years of sewing and cooking. Despite these imposed stipulations, Sumner established and maintained as its predominant emphasis college-preparatory coursework. By 1940, four distinct curriculum tracks had been developed: college preparatory, general arts, commercial arts and a general course or normal training course (teacher training). Courses were divided into two groups, and students were required to take twelve credits in Group 1 and six or eight credits in Group 2. This scheduling procedure came into being in 1939, at the same time the new building at Eighth and Oakland Avenue opened. The two course groupings utilized are provided below.

21 S. P. Davis, "The History of Sumner High School." Unpublished, 1935.

Group 1

English I, II, II; Algebra I, II; Geometry I, II; Business Arithmetic; Latin I, II, III; French I, II, III; History I, II; Civics; General Science; Physiology; Botany; Biology; Physics, Chemistry; Psychology; Bookkeeping; Shorthand I, II

Group 2

Manual Training I, II, III; Auto Mechanics; Mechanical Drawing; Cooking I, II; Sewing I, II, III; Physical Training; Public Speaking; Music; Orchestra; Typewriting I, II

Figure 4.6 Evolution of Curricula

School Year	Courses Offered (Courses added to the original curriculum are in successive years.)
1905	English, Geometry, Algebra, Greek, Roman and American History, Civics, Botany, Physics
1908-1909	Shorthand, Typewriting, Bookkeeping (basketball, baseball and football added from efforts of G.B. Buster)
1919-1920	Physical Education, French, Typing
1923	Spanish, English II, III, IV, Business Arithmetic, French II & III, American History, Chemistry, Biology, Typewriting II, Shop Practice, Auto Mechanics, Woodwork I, II Sumner Division of Junior College Normal School
1924-1925	U.S. Constitution as a result of Kansas law requiring schools to teach the Constitution Botany, European History
1927-1928	Journalism
1928-1929	Commercial Law
1931-1932	Economics, Mechanical Drawing I-III

continued on page 64…

...*continued from page 63*

School Year	Courses Offered (Courses added to the original curriculum are in successive years.)
1905	English, Geometry, Algebra, Greek, Roman and American History, Civics, Botany, Physics
1908-1909	Shorthand, Typewriting, Bookkeeping (basketball, baseball and football added from efforts of G.B. Buster)
1919-1920	Physical Education, French, Typing
1923	Spanish, English II, III, IV, Business Arithmetic, French II & III, American History, Chemistry, Biology, Typewriting II, Shop Practice, Auto Mechanics, Woodwork I, II Sumner Division of Junior College Normal School
1924-1925	U.S. Constitution as a result of Kansas law requiring schools to teach the Constitution Botany, European History
1927-1928	Journalism
1928-1929	Commercial Law
1931-1932	Economics, Mechanical Drawing I-III
1934-1935	Band music
1940	Cosmetology, Machinists Trades, Vocational Carpentry, Upholstery

In the 1939–1940 school guide, there were increased vocational and commercial subjects from which students could choose. In the aftermath of the Great Depression, the school curricula became diversified as a practical means of preparing students to earn a living and pay college tuition. Mirroring academics in the quality of instruction, the shop and commercial classes were also first class throughout the years.

During the 1954 to 1956 academic years, only three courses were added to the selection of courses: business law, transcription, and crafts. In 1960, there were a number of courses added: science survey, photography, vocations, and business administration. The selection of courses for art was expanded to include elementary art, advanced art, and general art. In addition, health and basic education were also added. In 1976, the auto mechanics teacher, Mr. Ed Lenheim, reported that the class earned between $500 and $600 each month. From picking up junk autos that were donated by the community, selling base parts to be pulverized, and keeping the usable parts for recycling, the class was able raise money for the program. Leadership and team work were part and parcel of the curriculum that taught students to perform tune-ups, do brake systems replacement and repair, do exhaust system repairs, and analyze and fix other vital functions that resulted in overall auto repair.

The categorical subject areas associated with the college-preparatory curriculum consisted of English, literature, mathematics, foreign language, art, music, and social studies. On a regular basis, course offerings under those headings were changed at the discretion of the school, pursuant to approval by the Kansas City, Kansas School Board. Sumner, however, always placed considerable emphasis on offering literature as an area of study. Thus, throughout its history, the school exposed Spartans to such brilliant writers and thinkers as Shakespeare, Hawthorne, Milton, Donne, Langston Hughes, Khayyam, Thoreau, and Kipling. This exposure taught valuable character-building concepts while delivering messages about human nature, dignity, honor, the pursuit of truth, and other facets of life. Students were made to analyze and dissect classical writings, uncovering their timeless truisms and mythological inferences. Such exercises were instrumental in imparting new ways of thinking and gaining insight into the foibles of humankind. The areas of mathematics and science were also emphasized, particularly as a result of the educational orientation of Principal Hodge. During his thirty-five year stay, Hodge insured the existence of substantive coursework in the general sciences. Those efforts were sustained throughout the decades and culminated in the winning of numerous first place science fair awards during the 1950s.

POSTSECONDARY EDUCATION OPTIONS

Under the helm of John Hodge, Sumner expanded educational opportunities in two other important areas: a normal school (for the training of future teachers) and the Sumner Junior College Division, which existed from 1923 to 1951.[22] The normal school course of study prepared a significant number of Sumner graduates to become teachers in segregated Kansas City, Kansas, schools. Mr. Hodge was appointed assistant dean of the Sumner Junior College Division, and curriculum requirements were identical to those of the Kansas City, Kansas Junior College (prior to 1951, exclusively for whites). Successful completion of courses from the Sumner Junior College Division was credited at colleges and universities throughout the state. No tuition was charged, and all residents who completed high school were eligible to enroll in either postsecondary course of study offered at the high school.

> In 1951, the Kansas City Kansas Junior College at Ninth and State opened its doors for blacks to attend. We did, reluctantly. We were not met with open arms, but many obstacles. However, we surpassed their expectations of us because we excelled them in most classes. Henry Curry graduated with top honors in May 1953 as magna cum laude. We were very proud that May evening! Thanks to Principal Hodge and faculty for their encouragement.
>
> — Opal Lorene Toombs Marks, Class of 1951

Figure 4.7 Science Class (1921)

---

22 Sumner Courier. November 15, 1923. 1 (1, 2): 1.

Figure 4.8 Biology Class (1940)

Figure 4.9 Clothing Class (1940s)

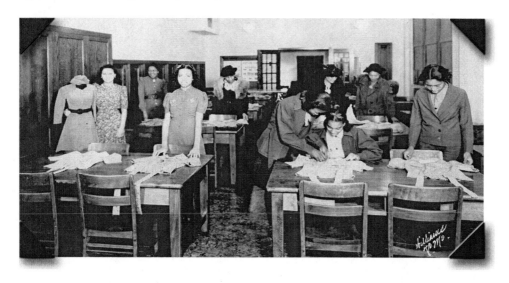

Figure 4.10 Science Fair 1954

Top Winners in Science Fair

Daniel Hughes Wilson, sophomore, received first place in the Greater Kansas City Science fair for his exhibit, "The Meson and Nuclear Forces" last April.

Shirlee Kay Ross, junior, won second place with her exhibit, a tiny electric organ which she designed.

Sumner's contestants competed against 608 other high school students with Daniel receiving the top score of 94 and Shirlee, 92.

Also, winning scholarship priorities were Marvin Knight, senior with his titrimeter, securing first place in this category; Benjamin Evans, senior seventh place with his electroplating exhibit; and Beverly Wallace, senior, thirteenth, with her exhibit of plastics.

Wilma Baskin, junior, with her oscillograph, would probably have won sixth place had her exhibit not needed adjusting, which delay ran over the deadline.

R. R. Mansfield was teacher sponsor of Daniel's exhibit; W. J. Smith, Shirlee's; W. W. Boone, Marvin's, Benjamin's and Beverly's; and W. J. Smith, Wilma's.

In 1952 Arvey Andrews received third top honor with his oscilloscope.

Daniel and Shirlee competed in the National Science Fair, May 7-9 at Oak Ridge, Tennessee, together with the third place winner.

The Kansas City Star, sponsor of the local fair, sent the three contestants with their exhibits to Oak Ridge.

Figure 4.11 Science Fair 1956

TOPS IN SCIENCE FAIR

Beckwith Horton and Myrna Thomas, top winners in the Greater Kansas City, Science Fair, receive an autograph from Miss Nadine Powell, their T. W. A. hostess, before boarding a plane to Chicago in route to compete in the National Science Fair in Cleveland.

Figure 4.12 Science Fair 1958

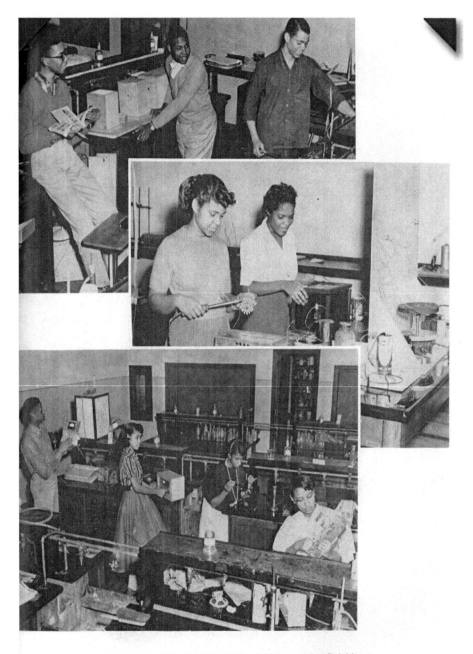

PREPARING FOR SCIENCE FAIR--Students putting finishing touches on projects are top photo-Lelond Holbert, George Ragsdale, and Michael Rogers. Center-Mary Barker and Shirley Baker. Bottom-Elmer Jackson, Jo Anne Holbert, Gerry Weaver, and Yvonne Jackson.

CO-CURRICULAR ACTIVITIES

I have met African-American males from all over the country. I was surprised to discover that very few were exposed to the same quality of experiences and role models that we had at Sumner.

— John Young, Class of 1964

The value of co-curricular programs and activities was recognized early in the school's history and continually expanded over the years. As a complement to the curricula, Sumner provided numerous venues where students could further grow and develop. Under the component of co-curricular activities, students were provided opportunities to compete, apply skills and talents developed in the classroom, learn social etiquette, and gain exposure not possible in the traditional classroom. Faculty members organized and sponsored these activities and programs, which involved expending significant time and energy outside of regular school hours. No additional monetary compensation was provided to the faculty for these efforts. In cases of competitive events—such as science fairs, band competitions, vocal music festivals, debates, and sports—Sumner students frequently excelled.

The high standards that were an integral part of all contests cultivated character, discipline, and stamina. Of particular note is Sumner's record of success in the Greater Kansas Science Fair Competitions. These competitions began in 1952, after the mayor, academic leaders, businesses, and the public backed the New International Science Fair movement. Students from Kansas City, Kansas, and Kansas City, Missouri, competed fiercely. Among the white and other black competitors, Sumner students consistently demonstrated their science acumen; they brought home multiple "grand championship" awards.

Spartan winners from the first decade of entries were Arvey Andrews (1952); Daniel Wilson and Shirlee Ross (1953); Barbara Skinner (1954); Jere DeLee Dando who attended Sumner and transferred to Shawnee Mission (1954); Beckwith Horton and Myrna Loy (1955); John Hodge and Norma Cole (1956); Patricia Caruthers (1957); and JoAnne Holbert (1958). The lack of publicity and recognition of Sumner High School as a leading competitor was cited by Professors Frank T. Manheim and Eckhard Hellmuth in the June/July 2006 issue of *USBE & Information Technology*. Fittingly, the article is titled, "Achievers Obscured by

History—Black High Schools Sumner and Lincoln Dominated Science Awards in Kansas City in the 1950s. So Why Doesn't Anybody Know About This?" (From 1952 to 1958, Mr. William W. Boone, Class of 1947, taught chemistry at Sumner and played an instrumental role in preparing students for science fairs. Mr. Boone subsequently was promoted to principal of Northeast Junior High School.)

Excluding athletic teams, some of the co-curricular organizations that were active at some time during the life of Sumner High School are:

Figure 4.13 *Selected Clubs and Organizations of Sumner*

Boys' Glee Club	Journalism Club
Chess Club	Madrigal Ensemble
Class Officers	Majorette Corps
Courier Staff	Cheerleader Squad
Debate Club	Pep Club
Dramatics Guild	Physics Club
Future Business Leaders	Quill and Scroll Honor Society
Future Homemakers	Splash Club
Future Teachers of America	Student Council
Girls' Glee club	Sumner High Band
Health Careers Club	Sumner High Choir
Hi-Y Club	Sumner Orchestra
Industrial Arts Club	Y-Teens
Jazz Band	

In addition to clubs sponsored by the school, there were popular social organizations that were outside of the school's purview. They were viewed by many as "pre" sororities and fraternities. Membership was selective, and keen competition existed among them. Club members learned and used Robert's Rules of Order. They planned and executed sophisticated social events, ranging from teas and fashion shows to plays and seasonal balls. Members learned to negotiate and carry out agreements of formal contracts as they secured impressive sites to hold their activities and borrowed clothes and paraphernalia to model and execute their ambitious plans. The Leader Clothing Store, Adler's Clothing Store, The Little Theater, the Pyramid Club, the Party House, and the Kansas City, Kansas, YWCA were a few well-known businesses that conducted regular transactions with these clubs. Families also took an active role in supporting the students by hosting meetings in their homes, where full-course dinners were served, and by supervising slumber parties, initiation rituals, and dance parties at regular intervals. Parents identified and functioned as seamstresses, bakers, and other service providers to implement the clubs' varied events.

During the early decades of the school, clubs for girls included Dardanella Girls, Les Travailleurs, and Arcencil Girls; clubs for boys included Nonpariel Club and Aufait Boys' Club. Toward the middle of the century, the clubs for girls were Les Charmantes Dames, Les Gaies Mademoiselles, and Les Jeunes Filles; Flamingos, Frocks, and Vireos were for the boys.

Figure 4.14   Orchestra 1918

Figure 4.15 Band (1921)

Figure 4.16 Hi-Y Club (1920s)

ATHLETICS

Of course, going to the football and basketball games was a social highlight. We always had a tremendous basketball team. Our football team was great my tenth-grade year.

— Jacques Barber, Class 1968

It would be no exaggeration to suggest that an entire book could be written about the athletic endeavors of Sumner High School and their unifying effect. The purpose of this section, however, is not to cover any co-curricular topic in that detail but to provide sufficient evidence of the vital contributions of these activities. A "snapshot" view of the basketball teams from 1954 to 1974 is presented in figure 4.9. This twenty-year period is representative of other eras in which pride and a competitive spirit were fostered within the school and the surrounding community. This point is illustrated, for example, with Sumner's win of the 1942 National Negro Basketball Championship in Durham, North Carolina. Between 1954 and 1973, 393 basketball games were played, with 292 wins and 101 losses. In sports, this 75 percent win record is phenomenal, one to be envied. These successes rallied the support of students, teachers, administrators, and the community giving, all concerned not only a sense of pride but also an enviable reputation throughout the state and beyond. The legacy gained was a catalyst for teams in successive years to aspire to even greater heights.

Figure 4.17 Girls Basketball Team (1923)

Figure 4.18 Boys Basketball Team (1922)

Figure 4.19 Football Team (1922)

Figure 4-20   Football Coaches over the Years

1907	Charles Star (assisted by J.P. King and G.B. Buster)
1923 - 1933	A.T. Edwards, Athletic Director (1926-1927), (assisted by Mr. Williams)
1933 - 1941	James Thatcher (served in the army after 1941)
1942 – 1944	Paul Mobiley
1945 – 1953	James Thatcher
1954	Onan Burnett
1954 – 1958	William Bradley
1958 – 1962	Gerald Hall
1963 – 1965	Cleveland Jones
1967 – 1969	William Spencer
1970 – 1974	Felton Denham
1975 – 1976	Michael Reed
1977	Lawrence Smith

Figure 4.21 Track Team (1940s)

Figure 4.22 Junior College Basketball Team (1937)

Figure 4.23   Notable Athletic Achievements

1905 ---	Boys Basketball
1906 ----	Four girls basketball teams formed
1907----	Boys Football started (Coached by Charles Star, J.P. King and G.B. Buster)
1942----	National Negro basketball champions (Coach, Kenneth Hill)
1967----	Wrestling team formed (Coach, Chester Pittman)
1967----	Baseball team formed (Coach, Roy Flook)
1969----	Boys State basketball champions (Coach, Roy Flook)
1973----	Girls track team formed
1975-----	Girls varsity and Jr. varsity basketball teams formed (Coach, Winnie Ayers)
1975----	Girls volleyball team formed (Coach, Jean Chambers)
1975 thru 1977-----	Boys State Outdoor Track Champions (Coach, Cecil Carter)

SUMNER BASKETBALL TEAMS
1954-1974

1954 (18-3)
3rd in Regionals

Willie Hatton
Stephen Carter
Ronald Hamilton
Wendell Henderson
Montell Roberts
Jerry Weeden
Clarence Henderson
Wardell Anderson
Harvey Murphy
Aubry Singleton
Charles Davis
Walter Young
Don Kimbrough
Alvin Jones

1955 (9-9)

Charles Weems
Charles Davis
Walter Young
Don Kimbrough
Andrew Henderson
John Roberson
Charles Thomas
Thomas McClain
Maynard Keith
Alvin Jones
Craig Hall
Benoyd Meyers
John Yates
Robert Stephens
Harvey Murphy

1956 (14-5)
3rd in Regionals

Andrew Henderson
Frank Murphy
Clark Bazy
Alvin Jones
Charles Thomas
Tim Hayden
Craig Hall
John Roberson
Charles Weems
Maynard Keith
Benoyd Meyers
Mike Richardson
Nevernon Roberson

1957 (4-10)

Fred Johnson
Benoyd Meyers
Kermit Kitchen
Adolph Wilson
Sam Malone
Michael Richardson
Wallace Franklin
Nevernon Roberson
Fred Robinson
John Keith
Herman Mitchem
Ernest Fant
Alvin Fant

1958 (13-3)

Frank Henderson
John Keith
Ernest Moore
Alvin Fant
William Robinson
Herman Mitchem
Michael Rogers
Sam Malone
Adolph Wilson
Ernest Turner
Tommy Roberts
Gerald Milton

1959 (15-5)
Regional Champs
2nd in State-Wichita

Robert Smith
Sam Malone
Martin Grizzell
Alvin Fant
Adolph Wilson
Harold Smallwood
James Hill
Ernest Moore
Ernest Turner
William Coleman
Alverns Martin
Perry Pitchlyn

1960 (8-9)

William Perry
William Coleman
Otis Brewer
Louis Plummer
Lemuel Norman
Ronald Holly
Samuel Cofield
Charles Payne
Luther Hurt
William Collins
Herman Watson
Brian Montgomery

1961 (10-9)
Regional Champs
State-Wichita

John Collins
Otis Brewer
Samuel Cofield
Shelby Johnson
William Starks
Richard Dumas
Lemuel Norman
Donald Hibler
Andrew Smith
Kenneth Cloud
William Owens
Herman Watson
Eurvin Williams
Ronald Holly

1962 (19-2)
2nd in Regionals

John Collins
Eurvin Williams
Sylvester Wimbley
Donald Nash
Adolphus Favors
Bertram Caruthers
Bill Owens
Richard Dumas
Kenneth Cloud
Donald Hibler
Clifford Hobbs
William Starks
Herman Watson

1963 (13-6)

Rudolph Thompson
Samuel Ward
Kenneth Harris
Benjamin Johnson
Dwight Henderson
Lee James
Claude Baker
Ernest Lewis
McArthur Hall
Kenneth Cloud
Erroll Robinson
Willie Dixon
Terrell Jackson

1964 (12-6)

Edward Bell
Lee James
Rudolph Thompson
Kenneth Harris
Ernie Lewis
Erroll Robinson
Willie Dixon
Amos McCluney
Donald Moore
Michael Sanders
William White
Will Carrol
Curtis Long
Kenneth Fouse
Kenneth Nash

1965 (18-2)
2nd in Regionals

Curtis Long
Will Carroll
William White
Kenneth Fouse
Donald Moore
Lawrence Williams
Ernest Lewis
Erroll Robinson
Kenneth Nash
Kenneth Harris
Robert Nance
Michael Sanders

continued on page 80…

...continued from page 79

1966(15-5)
3rd in Regionals

Will Carrol
Robert White
William White
Heiskell Jackson
Kenneth Fouse
Dwight Hatchett
Curtis Carter
Gary Byers
Gerald Ellison
Ronald Harland
Robert Nance
Amos McCluney

1967 (14-7)
2nd in Regionals

Curtis Carter
Heiskell Jackson
Gary Byers
Ronald Harland
Leonard Gray
Don Franklin
William Weaver
Paul Graham
Robert Jones
Rufus Boykins
Paul Richardson
Nate Smith
Don Baskin
Herbert Simmons
Rufus Caruthers

1968 (18-2)
3rd in Regionals

Zachary Townsend
Rufus Caruthers
Lefelt Jackson
Don Frnaklin
Paul Graham
Robert Jones
Hurbert Simmons
Nate Smith
Leonard Gray
David Berry
Brian Rollins
William Weaver

1969 (23-0)
Regional Champs
State Champs-Wichita

Robert Ford
Anthony Glen
Don Young
Zachary Townsend
James Drew
John Lee
Nathaniel Smith
Leonard Gray
Karl Berry
Brian Rollins
James Jones
Rufus Caruthers
Lefelt Jackson
Paul Graham
Jerry Houston
Grover Edwards

1970 (18-5)
Regional Champs
4th in State - Emporia

Donnie Young
James Drew
Brian Rollins
Karl Berry
Grover Edwards
Bob Ford
Daryel Garrison
James Caruthers
Rodney Redic
Frank Hyrne
Dwayne Hill
Floyd Stevenson
Eddie David
Dennis Hill

1971 (21-2)
Regional Champs
3rd in State-Manhattan

Dennis Hill
James Caruthers
Daryel Garrison
Eddie Davis
Michael Bailey
Rodney Redic
Frank Hyrne
James Townsend
Joel Hibler
Ronald Robinson
Michael Harris
Bruce Johnson
Dwayne Hill

1972 (19-11)
2nd in Regionals

Rodney Tolfree
Eddie Harold
James Townsend
Michael Bailey
Joel Hibler
William Carter
Ronald Scroggins
Curtis Jones
Bert Hendricks
Dwayne Hill
James Caruthers
Bruce Johnson
Ronnie Robinson

1973 (11-10)
Regional Champs
State - Wichita

Rodney Tolfree
Merie Johnson
Bert Hendricks
Michael Bailey
Joel Hibler
Ronald Scroggins
William Carter
Donald Easterwood
Kevin Fouse
Willie Evans
Frankie Davenport
Mike Maddox

1974

Paul Mitchell
William Carter
Ronald Scroggines
Kevin Fouse
Bert Hendricks
Mike Jimmerson
Ronald Henderson
Chester Powell
Mike Maddox
Jeffrey Jones
Keith Townsend
Myron Johnson
Anthony Harris
Alfredo Monroe
Albert McConnell

Figure 4.25 Early Sumner Trophies

HIGH STANDARDS AND EXPECTATIONS

The faculty, parents, and community were all encouraging and insisting that we outperform and achieve more than students enrolled in white schools.

— Theodore Madison, Class of 1948

While high standards and expectations are factors that kept Sumner together, they are very difficult to quantify. Their effects, however, were far-reaching and evident in every endeavor. Parents, administrators, faculty, and support personnel worked in concert to convey and enforce such standards as: mandatory daily school attendance; swift and certain punishment for non-adherence to school rules; respectful and orderly student conduct at all times; participation of the total school community in keeping the premises clean and clutter-free; conformance to long-standing standards of excellence in all school assemblies, theatrical presentations, and musicals. The constant striving to achieve excellence reaped rewards for individual students as well as for the school as a whole.   There appeared to be an operational code of conduct among the teachers themselves, in that high instructional standards were passed from teacher to teacher in specific subject areas. For example, starting with Scottie P. Davis in the English Department, the legacy for outstanding academic instruction was taken up by Rebecca Bloodworth; in chemistry and science, William Boone passed the baton to Paul Mobiley and Webster Gaylord; in mathematics, George Green set the tone for William Smith and Clarence Turpin; Robert Clark and Leon Brady followed the path blazed by T. H. Reynolds in music; in industrial arts, C. H. Mowbray set the standard upheld by Charles Terry; Greene B. Buster threw down the gauntlet for Edward Beasley in American History. Surely, the careful selection of teachers to replace those who departed their posts (often to retire) was a factor in sustaining quality instruction. But it was not the only factor. The impact of the trust and esteem paid by parents, students, and the community, along with pressures to maintain such regard, must have also compelled the faculty to maintain their high standards of instruction.

There were two crucial principles underlying the setting of standards above and beyond the realm of mediocrity: (1) high regard for excellence, and (2) belief in the ability of students to achieve at superior levels in multiple endeavors. The standards utilized by the faculty were identical to the ones that were imposed on them when they were students. Moreover, teachers must have seen themselves (years earlier) in the faces and backgrounds of those they taught. Accordingly, they knew what was accomplishable with hard work and perseverance. To believe in the value of striving for excellence merely for the sake of attaining excellence, without career opportunities and monetary rewards, speaks to the limitless stamina of those who focused on excelling. It is one thing to expect benefits from persistent practice or study when the rewards are visible today. But how drastically different it was seven decades ago, when there were only a few blacks reaping the benefits of their labor.

It was accepted by the students, as well as instructors, that one's socioeconomic background was irrelevant to one's capacity to learn. Regardless of one's economic station, the culture of Sumner mandated high levels of achievement and deportment. Whether in sports, science, industrial trades, music, or oratory, the standards were set high for all. It was believed that the acquisition of knowledge and skills would result in a fulfilling life and could be ultimately transformed into enhanced earning power.

It is doubtful that the standards of conduct and academic performance would have been set so high for students unless there was also the general expectation of their attainment. It is astounding to consider how expectations, whether set high or low, are manifested in what is commonly known as the "self-fulfilling prophecy." That is, once expectations are implicitly and explicitly incorporated into a culture, those expectations become manifest. What is expected is realized. High standards and expectations at Sumner were integral in holding the school together.

Figure 4.26 David Henderson First to Win Essay Contest

THE SUMNERIAN

FRESHMAN WINS GREAT HONOR FOR SUMNER HIGH SCHOOL

NO MAN ever proves higher than the value he sets upon himself. The upper classmen have always thought of the freshmen as being their inferiors. But, David Henderson, a freshman, proved that the freshmen were not inferior and he brought honor and fame to himself, his parents, his school and his class.

Opportunity is all that we need to show to the world that we possess potential capacity of intellect and are capable of performing any task well.

The Chamber of Commerce held their annual essay contest. The subject was entitled, "Our Greatest Opportunity," and was submitted to all of the schools of Kansas City, Kansas. The pupils were divided into three groups and our class was entered in Group B.

David Henderson submitted the best essay in Group B from all of the schools in the city and this won for Sumner High School a silver cup and entitled David to a membership in the Chamber of Commerce.

Can we ever think of Sumner without thinking of David Henderson? No! David won for himself the distinction of being the first negro in the Chamber of Commerce. He gained for the freshmen the honor of being the class who brought victory to Sumner. He gained for Sumner the esteem of the community and of the competitive schools.

David Henderson has made an excellent record this year. We are looking forward to the time when we may point to greater victories that he has won. I am sure that all are willing to acknowledge that Sumner has been made better for having had David Henderson as a student.

CHAPTER FIVE

MEMORIES, REFLECTIONS, AND PERSPECTIVES

My Sumner experience was the foundation for my life's journey in a positive direction... Dear ole Sumner High is one of my favorite memories.

— Paulyne Patterson Depp, Class of 1948

Memories and reflections filtered through time, experience, and maturity allow us to see things from a different perspective. They take us to places where the factual accounting of history may not always go. They also give us permission to revisit, review, and reassess where we were then and where we are now. They allow us to look back on things that matter and to look ahead on things that will endure. It is through these dual lenses that the reader is encouraged to enter this chapter. So whether the reader is a Sumner alumnus or a first-time visitor to the Sumner experience, he will find something that will touch him. For the memories, reflections, and perspectives, found here, are both personal and universal.

When it comes to reflecting on old high school memories, Sumner is undoubtedly like any other high school across the country: it only takes a "remember when" starter to fuel a conversation that could last well into the evening. Equally fascinating is the range of interpretations about one single event that could ignite a debate that could carry on from one reunion to the next. Yet, within those memories are some of Sumner's finest moments which, from the writing team's perspective, are integral to its sacred archives. So, whether they are truths, half-truths, or just nostalgic imaginations, they reveal cherished secrets about what made Sumner special. On a larger and very realistic scale, they reflect common themes of Spartans' high school experiences.

The Sumner Writing Team set out to accomplish a daunting, yet achievable task, of documenting the existence of an extraordinary high school over a period of seventy-three years with two realities in mind. First, the Sumner story had to be a collective enterprise; a person, team, or committee could in no way do justice to the recount without input from many. Second, the story had to include both historical facts and data combined with personal memories to give context to forces that influenced the evolution of Sumner High School. Thus, this section contains the factual, the funny, and the familiar. The objectives of this chapter are to share some lasting impressions of alumni, identify central themes that cut across classes and generations, and articulate a central message for us today and for generations to come.

From William "Red" Starks '62

I was on a flight from Denver to Philadelphia on the now extinct TWA, which in those days meant a stop in Kansas City or St. Louis. I noticed a petite, well-groomed, and professionally attired woman coming down the aisle toward me; she had boarded in Kansas City. I didn't think much of it as… I had been out of Kansas City for many years, and she could have been from anywhere. By chance, her seat was the window seat next to my aisle seat… I am unable to recall what sparked our interactions, but at some point, I asked the nature of her travels. She answered that she was in Kansas City visiting relatives and was headed back to her workplace. It seems she held some position of importance, the title of which evades my recollection … I was singularly impressed that this unassuming lady, whose name also escapes me, was employed at the United States consulate in Libya… She revealed herself as a member of the [Sumner] class of 1955. We had a most entertaining time all the way to Philadelphia, where I got off and she continued on to North Africa.

I cite this incident as one of many I've had over the years. My career allowed me to travel across the country and I have met… so many products of Sumner High doing so many things that it started me to musing about something that, while being experienced, was taken for granted. Not until the late 1960s and early 1970s, when encountering other black people who were from many other parts of the country, did it begin to sink in with me that **something special had gone on in northeast Kansas City, Kansas**… for me and many others, the culmination was the experience at Sumner High School.

LASTING IMPRESSIONS

The following anecdotes reflect experiences, perspectives, and priorities of the era.

From Loris Vincson Jones, Class of '45
(taken from *Family Histories 1905–1978*)

In reflection on my years spent at Sumner High, I fondly remember the teachers, activities, and my classmates of 1945 and friends of other classes. I can vividly remember the short walks to school, as I lived within a few blocks. I was constantly running to be on time. My favorite classes were history, Latin, and journalism.

I can vividly remember Mr. Curry, Latin instructor, who was very serious, cool in demeanor, but rich in imparting his philosophy of life. So often he would look over to our side of the room when my friends and I seemed engaged in talking quietly (Anna Pearl) rather than giving him our undivided attention. He would admonish us by saying, "All right! A rolling stone gathers no moss." We would immediately lean on his every word.

Mr. Buster wasted no class time, but embarked upon the task of imparting as much knowledge and wisdom as he could with the allotted time. He stated in one of his memorable dialogues that young ladies, in thinking about marriage, [should] concern [themselves] with whether the man loves, cares for [them], and whether he has the ability and the willingness to make a living for [them]. How wise that advice was, even though we didn't realize the significance of his words until years later. He cautioned us to make a shift if we did have the real item and would challenge our minds to think in terms of, "What if I didn't have?"

Miss Hoffman's class in journalism was so enjoyable as she guided [us] into the many ways of writing articles for the school newspaper, the *Sumner Courier*. In 1945, my letter to Second Lt. Elihu Moore from our journalism class won Sumner High School an award from the U.S. Treasury Department.

In my final tribute of memorable teachers, [I] can hardly leave out the tenacity of Scottie P. Davis, who demanded excellence in [one's] work as she, herself, gave so much.

All too soon those glorious years ended, and I was selected as one of the speakers for our commencement. My speech involved the utilization of air travel in that one would be able to have breakfast in New York and dinner in London. My father, the late Robert B. Vincson, delivered the invocation. He was the assistant pastor of Metropolitan Baptist Temple, Ninth and Washington Boulevard.

Mr. Hodge was so encouraging as a principal and would often stop me in the hall and ask what [I was] adding to [my] archives today. It showed that he was very aware of the various honors or events that [students] were involved in and was there to say congratulations and keep striving.

From Quintelle Davis Thatcher, Class of '46

Sumner was indeed a special experience. The teachers were more than just teachers: they seemed to really be concerned about their students, even though the pay was not that great. In more recent years, both of my daughters have expressed what their early years at Sumner High School meant to them. They have shared many times how much they really learned while attending Sumner. One daughter now teaches in a community college, and she writes her own course of study. This is probably due to early teachings at Sumner.

From Virginia L. Freeman Ferguson, Class of '47
(taken from *Family Histories 1905–1978*)

"We will sing *its worth* throughout the earth, the name of Sumner, dear ole Sumner; sing the name of Sumner High!"

My Sumner experience has come to mean legacy, and one of the many ways that legacy gets translated is through its school cheers and through its school song. I sang these last bars of the Sumner song to introduce a workshop presentation, "What It Meant to Have Been a Student at Sumner High School." I also asked the workshop participants if they knew or could recall any or all of their high school song. Some said they really didn't know if their school really had a song. Others, well, it became a very real challenge to think seriously about the impact of one's high school song. However, I believe that when we think of Sumner and "its worth," we think of many unmatched records of academic excellence, extraordinarily well-prepared faculties, and many, many wonderful students. Also we think of ongoing administrative stability but also administrative vision. For Sumner, until it officially closed as a high school, "its worth" meant having and maintaining a clear educational mission. So, when I think of Sumner, I think of this kind of indelible legacy. The aura of this specialness is what makes us all Sumnerites, a legacy never to be removed.

From Richard M. Hopkins, Class of '52 (taken from *Family Histories 1905–1978*)

I arrived at Sumner High School in the fall of 1950. At that time, I had two specific goals in mind. My first goal was to make my mother happy by graduating. Secondly, my goal was to come out of this experience prepared to enter the work world in some venue other than Kansas City, Kansas; preferably the U.S. Navy.

In September of 1951, I entered the vocational carpentry class under the tutelage of Mr. Charles Terry. To my surprise, the demeanor of his class was as disciplined as was my English class the year before under Mrs. Hoffman. This was a perfect and ideal atmosphere for learning. Mr. Terry gave respect and demanded it in return. Motivated by two goals, I quickly worked myself into the position as one of the class leaders.

In the two years that I was a student in Mr. Terry's vocational carpentry class, I learned as much as anyone could learn about home construction. We built a scale model home in the classroom during the winter months, and during the spring, we ventured out into the community and remodeled baths and kitchens. At the end of the year, we disassembled the classroom house, board by board. By using this technique, we not only learned the principles of construction, we also learned techniques that are beneficial in remodeling and rehabilitation. I was to learn later how critical this training was to all of my successes later in life.

My senior year I went out for and made the Sumner basketball team. My employer, Mr. Maslan, threatened to fire me because I could not be there at 3:00 PM. I turned in my uniform and left the team. That was the end of anything but school hour activities. When I graduated from Sumner, I had what amounts to an A average in the vocational carpentry class.

In April 1952, I turned 18 and immediately volunteered to join the U.S. Navy. With all of my vocational carpentry training, my dream was to be a member of the navy's Construction Battalion (the famed CBs). In 1952, all the practices of segregation and discrimination were still in place. There was not room in the Construction Battalion for a young "colored boy" from Kansas City, Kansas', Sumner High, his training notwithstanding. My next choice was [to be] an electrician, an integral part of home construction. The answer again was no. The recruiters wanted me to enter the navy as an apprentice steward, "a servant" to the officers. My reply was, "Absolutely not."

Before I would commit myself to that humiliation, I would join the air force. With that statement, I turned to walk away. The recruiter called me back and agreed to allow me to enter as a seaman apprentice. My older brother, who joined the navy during World War II, had warned me of the navy's racist practices. I knew as a seaman apprentice, at the very least, I had a fighting chance. So I enlisted.

From Wilma Baskins Scroggins, Class of '54 (taken from *Family Histories 1905–1978*)

Sumner became a tradition in my family. I grew up looking forward to the Sumner aura of eccentric but excellent teachers, because all of my sisters and brothers had attended before me.

The Eurskin and Ethel Baskin family moved from Armourdale, Kansas to Wyandotte in 1928 to avoid their oldest daughter, Emma Louise, having to ride the streetcar early in the mornings alone at such a young age from Armourdale to the new junior high school, Northeast, located at Fourth and Troup. The move to 623 Winona in the northeast of Kansas City, Kansas meant that all of the Baskin children and some of their children attended Sumner High School.

Emma Louise Smith (1933), Eurskin Baskin (1936), Walter Baskin, and Retta Mayes (1939) all graduated from Sumner at the Ninth and Washington Building. Creasy Estell (1942) was with the first class that attended the new Sumner building at Eighth and Oakland in 1940. She started there the second semester of the tenth grade. Rosafrieda Johnson was scheduled to graduate in 1944, but she and a large number of Sumner students completed the twelfth grade in the newly formed Sumner School and graduated in 1943. There was no graduation ceremony, however; they were just given a diploma. Betty B. Pearson (1947), Eugene Baskin (1949), and I, Wilma Scroggins, completed the list of the Baskin children who were Spartans.

Both my late husband, Donald Scroggins (1953), and I graduated from Sumner High School. Two of our children, Ronald Scroggins and Pamela Scroggins Banks, also graduated Sumner High School, but not as we knew it. By their time in the 1970s, Sumner had been "integrated," although that only applied to the teachers, because there were a few white faculty in administrative positions. Donald played drums in the Sumner band and marched in the traditional American Royal Parade each fall. Our son, Ronald, determined to follow in his tradition, and although not an official member of the band class, played the sousaphone in the American Royal Parade while in the tenth grade. Ronald was an honor student and also lettered in Spartan basketball. Our daughter, Pamela, an honor student and a cheerleader, also marched in the American Royal Parade.

Our two younger children, Richard Scroggins and Ursula Scroggins Youngblood, did not attend Sumner as a result of the new government desegregation suit, which also closed Northeast and relegated Sumner into history. Richard was in the class most adversely affected, because they were transported to Arrowhead in the middle of their [junior] high experience. Although eligible, neither he nor Ursula chose to attend the resulting academy, which had abandoned all relevance to our Sumner heritage.

From Alice Yates Banks, Class of '61
(taken from _Family Histories 1905–1978_)

Growing up on Ninth and Freeman, down the street from Sumner High School, all I could think of was that someday I would attend this big, beautiful school. My sister, who is eight years my senior, took me to basketball games, plays, etc. at Sumner when I was a small child. I heard about the legendary teachers before I got there—teachers such as Rebecca Bloodworth, William Smith, John Henderson, Clarence Turpin, and Mr. William Boone, and, of course, Mr. S. H. Thompson, principal. I heard much talk about the notorious Mr. Taylor, the biology teacher, who put students out of class if you did not know a biology fact. He also made you write the answer to the question you missed one hundred times, which assured you would know it the next time he asked the question. I had to write a lot of biology facts for my brother, John, while I was still in elementary school.

When I entered Sumner as a sophomore in 1958, I felt I had arrived. I finally had an opportunity to walk those hallowed halls and meet the teachers I had heard so much about. They were tough, but they cared about us. They made us stretch and encouraged us to reach our potential.

I took the basic college-preparatory classes as well as business subjects. My mother always told me to have a marketable skill. I enjoyed all the classes that I took at Sumner but especially the business subjects. I had excellent teachers: Alice Bennigan, Vivian Graves, and Mary Calhoun. I admired them so much that I decided to become a business teacher. The highlight of my teaching career was teaching bookkeeping, shorthand, secretarial practice, business machines, business law, and typing in the same rooms where I had been a student. I taught at Sumner from 1972 to 1978.

Unfortunately, along with Gloria Brown Johnson and Brenda Wood Isom, I watched as the workmen destroyed the concrete high school, leaving only [the name] Sumner over the east door entrance of the building. We were distraught, and we must have looked it, because the workers said, "Sorry, ladies, I'm just doing my job." We were distraught, because we knew it was the end of a golden era. They were making way for the establishment of Sumner Academy of Arts and Science. Sumner was an academy long before the Board of Education changed its name. As a matter of fact, it should have been called Sumner University, which is how my brother-in-law, Lacy Banks, describes it being in the "good old days," when we were citizens of Spartan Town, U.S.A., the term coined by my husband, Jimmie Banks.

There were eight of us that entered Kansas State College of Pittsburg in the fall of 1961. After taking a placement test to determine which type of English class we would be enrolled in, all of us, because we had gone to Ms. Bloodworth, quizzed out of basic English that dealt with grammar, spelling, etc. We all were enrolled in the English composition class, the advanced writing class.

From Carolyn Buford Jones, Class of '62

All of us remember Mr. Thatcher's famous words, "Boy/young lady, I know your mama, your daddy, or somebody with whom you might have shared a gene or two." These teachers reminded us that they knew our genealogy, because they were a part of the neighborhoods where we lived. I can remember when I had to go to Mr. Johnson's house [French teacher] with my parents because my grade was slipping to a C. Accountability was a quick phone call away, and there was no question of who was "at fault" when a call went home. Yes, I lived in fear from time to time, but that fear also motivated me to be the best that I could be for fear of disappointing my teachers, my family, and yes, myself, as well as feeling embarrassed in front of my friends.

My memories of Sumner High School teachers range from those I felt did not treat all students with the same degree of fairness to those who didn't care who you were, only how well you performed in their class. I took two years of French at KU and barely opened a book, because I learned to conjugate verbs and repeat the French alphabet while marching around the classroom to a cadence of a ruler hitting, I think, a desk, a blackboard, or an unsuspecting body part. I think I am at least "smarter than a fifth grader" because of the five- and ten-minute runs to the library in order to research and take a pop quiz over some special period or person in history (Beasley). I learned to take notes, accurate notes that allowed me to pass freshman college classes where there were no less than two hundred students and where we were graded by our number (90562) instead of our name.

My final thoughts about Sumner focus on the relationships that have existed throughout the years—relationships that exist across specific graduating classes. My son graduated from Sumner Academy, my daughter from Schlagle High School. They have no concept of the reunions and the bond that we have maintained as Sumner High School graduates. It's wonderful to have a defined history, as well as memories of highly qualified teachers who demanded respect and discipline in our classrooms so that we could learn. Mr. Thompson could quiet an entire auditorium with just a glance and the movement of his head. What a wonderful feat! And, thank you Ms. Bloodworth for making me so conscious of the need to grammatically critique all that I have written!

From Rose Thierry Sims, Class of '62

I entered Sumner as a sophomore in 1959 and graduated in 1962—an honor student, I might add, which even now feels pretty good to say. My years were busy and meaningful, cranking out, what I must tout, a darn good citizen—me. The highlights of my activities at Sumner included participation in the honor society, the varsity cheerleading squad, the Y-teens with Ms. Melba Hall as sponsor, the orchestra conducted by

Mr. Robert Clark, and the chorus under the director of Mr. Oyarma Tate, as well as various science and language clubs. Jo Marva Garth and I played around singing jazz with Dwight Foster on saxophone and a few visiting jazz artists on other instruments. In one of the yearbooks, it says that I wanted to become a teacher (a safe aspiration for a girl) and a concert pianist. I just about hit it—I teach English and French in high school, and piano in my private studio. Instead of a concert pianist, I'm a concert and opera singer.

From Arlana Joy Williams-Coleman, Class of '67 (taken from *Family Histories 1905–1978*)

My days at Sumner were very happy. I had a very active social life and enjoyed friendships that have lasted long past our time at Sumner. As I reflect on my life, I think two experiences at Sumner were of great benefit to me: 1. The clerical skills taught in Ms. Brooks' class allowed me to get my foot in the door at AT&T. When I was hired, I was competing against another Spartan for the job. We were both well equipped with the basic skills, but my ability to type and take shorthand gave me the edge for the job. 2. At Sumner, I was business manager for the *Courier* (school newspaper) and a member of the *Sumnerian* staff (yearbook). The skills learned in these extracurricular activities helped to develop my organizational skills.

My experiences at Sumner prepared me well for the future. I recall what Ms. Brooks wrote in my *Senior Memories Book*. "You have a wonderful personality." I believe this, combined with hard work, has served me well. I continued my education after Sumner and graduated magna cum laude from St. Mary College with a BS in business administration and public affairs. Upon completing my study at KCK Community College, in addition to receiving my AA in business management, I was inducted into the Phi Theta Kappa National Honor Fraternity.

I have been married to Larry Coleman [Class of '63] for over thirty-two years, and we have two children, Maurice (Myma) employed at BPU and vice president of the Schlagle Alumni Association, and Kimberlee (Othello), a third-year medical student at Kansas University.

From Jacques Barber, Class of '68

Mr. Charles "Baby Beef" Robinson was my geometry, Algebra II, trigonometry, and calculus teacher. He was also the coach of our chess team.

We had a formidable chess team. When we hosted a tournament, he would tell us that he was not spending money on trophies just to give them away to other schools. We always kept most of them. The chess tournaments usually had anywhere from six to nine boards, according to skill level, with first board being the most skilled players. One tournament was the day after a particularly hurtful basketball game. Normally, Mr. Robinson would not condone "loudtalking" or "selling wolf tickets" against other players. We did it all the time to each other during chess practice, however. During this particular tournament, we were still hurting from the night before, where the referees had been particularly blatant. Many of the chess team members were saying how they were going to put the "gimmieyo" on the other schools' players. During the game, yo' could hear all over the room, "Gimme yo' rook," "Gimmie yo' bishop," "Gimmie yo' knight," "Gimmie yo' queen." It was great. Mr. Robinson only made a passing admonition against the harassment. The tournament had seven boards, and we left with seven trophies.

CAPTURING THEMES

Throughout the seventy-three-year life of Sumner, there were common themes that helped Spartans remain focused. Personal values, ethnic isolation, and a collaborative relationship between the community and the school were critical variables in the formula of Sumner's success.

Theme 1: Personal values played a role in students' overall education: self-respect, honesty, and academic achievement. There was an understanding by students, teachers, parents, and everyone engaged in the teaching/learning process that, "You cannot be *as good as*, you have to be *better than*." That understanding produced a shared expectation of excellence. It resulted in teachers holding students accountable and responsible to exemplary codes of conduct and high learning standards. It could be seen in the way students dressed and carried themselves in and outside of the school and the way they treated their peers, teachers, and community members. The value of academic achievement was exemplified in the classrooms, where teachers facilitated stimulating discussions and created engaging lessons. Students were afraid to come to school ill-prepared because of fear of being embarrassed or getting an F, which was not removed from the record. Teachers assessed students comprehensively on the accuracy, thoroughness, and ability to support their answers. They were in accord in demanding high expectations from themselves and their students.

What life lessons and values did you learn from Sumner?

- Lucy Emma Barter Saunders '30: "Prayer before class began. Great feeling of belonging. Inspired to learn."

- Virginia Frances Curry '30: "Clean habits and a wholesome life are important in one's positive living."

- Verdaine Sanders Curry '39: "We were taught well that we could succeed at any school of higher learning."

- Gladys Harrison McClain '40: "A respect for education and educators is essential to appreciating and perpetuating our traditions of excellence."

- Arthur P. Allen '42: "We learned how to get along with people."

- Mildred Bradley '42: "Sumner instilled in me the true value of an education. All of my children graduated from Sumner with honors."

- Theodore (Ted) E. Madison '48: "We learned the importance of discipline … disrespect was not tolerated."

- Dorothy Kemp-Clark '48: "Love who you are, respect yourself and others, have a positive attitude. Sumner was a place of learning in an environment of caring, nurturing, discipline, character building, along with teaching reading, writing, and arithmetic. Having respect for one another; being like one big family."

- Alma Sue Richardson Hammonds '49: "But the current educational systems lack the values of the past."

- Adell Thompson '50: "They demanded that we excel. It wasn't a question if we would go to college."

- Patty M. Smith McManus '50: "They taught us how to achieve and take responsibility."

- Mary L. Northern '45: "Hard work pays off."

- Lawrence Langford Hoard '48: "Try to be all you can, when you go out into the world."

- Alma Sue Richardson Hammonds '49: "We learned to be supportive of others in the community."

- Adolphus T. Coleman '53: "We learned to recognize that our potential is only limited by ourselves."

- Bernice Long Johnson '58: "I was taught that I had value and that I could be somebody if I made wise decisions."

- William (Billy) Owens '62: "I often tell others that I received a 'private school' education at Sumner… all that brain power and talent was focused on providing an enriched social, sports, and academic environment that demanded excellence from all students. Sumner's staff reinforced positive moral values taught to and expected of students by parents, churches, and the community … Be the best you can at what you do. Never stop learning. Use what you have learned to help others. No matter what our circumstances, we are all brothers and sisters, and we can all do better if we work together and apply our God-given talents toward that end."

- Raymond L. Perkins, Jr. '62: "We learned to listen to people, to be objective in talking and understanding the other fellow's point of view."

- Adolphus Favors '62: "The first lesson I learned at Sumner was that I was going to college. I had no idea what I wanted to major in. I had no idea in what university I would matriculate. I didn't even know how to apply to college—but I knew that I was college bound. That notion was imbedded, implanted, submerged in my DNA early at Sumner High."

- Marion Paulette Mebane McBride '63: "We were taught fortitude; if you work at something, you get strength. Even if you don't succeed at that particular thing, there are lessons you learn along the way."

- Minnie Davis Givens '64: "I learned to take responsibility for my own future. I was told by several teachers that I could not sit back and wait for someone else to push me forward—that I had to take the initiative. This is when I began to excel in my grades. I also believed that I was ugly and no one liked me. It was teachers and faculty at Sumner who said to me, 'You are very beautiful, and don't you ever forget that.' I saw a different person the next time I looked into the mirror and learned to love myself and the way I looked, no matter what others thought. (Well, I may have taken that a little too far: I still think I look pretty hot at sixty-three.)"

- John Young '64: "If an individual invests in his own personal development, opportunities for achievement are almost unlimited."

- Howard A. Berry '64: "Mr. Eugene Taylor, truant officer, kept us focused, on track, and out of trouble. The custodial staff as well as the professional staff all cared for, monitored, and [encouraged] each and every student to achieve."

- Melanie A. Bailey '65: "We learned self-respect, responsibility, self-confidence, and a feeling of accomplishment."

- Calvin A. Flemings '66: "I gained a deep respect for the value of traditions, an appreciation for learning, and the importance and value of discipline in hard work. It also engendered within me a sense of pride as a black man."

- Brenda Joyce Harbin Jones '67: "All things are possible. The sky is the limit."

Theme 2: There was a collective awareness of our unique position, our ethnic isolation, in the city. As the only African-American high school in the city, we had a sense of being in the spotlight in everything we did, and we knew it. Every time Sumner was involved in activities outside of the school, we knew it could trigger a media event; we always knew what was at stake. Over time, we learned to walk the fine line between being fiercely competitive yet maintaining a sense of decorum. One little skirmish could reverse years of progress over night. There was a distant surveillance from all sectors of the community. There was the natural rivalry that came from other schools and from onlookers, both black and white, who watched with admiration, envy, or disdain. Whenever we left her hallowed halls, our teachers and administrators reminded us that we were Sumner ambassadors. We understood the rules of the game: nobody was giving anything away. We had to do well. We won local and state competitions in athletics, oratory, music, and academics because of skill and talent, not because of our color. In spite of prejudices levied against us because of our ethnicity, we prevailed.

- Emma Louise Baskin '33: "Sumner gave me a good foundational education to live in the segregated world into which we were born."

- Marian Singleton Jackson '34: "For me segregation was a plus. Teachers exerted themselves to provide all we needed as pre-college students."

- Thelma J. Weems Poole '50: "Faculty members did all they could to prepare you for a segregated world."

- William J. Strickland '53: "Expect the limitation of segregation but do not be limited by it."

- Valera Richmond Jefferson '62: "The reality of segregation inspired high standards permeating Sumner's staff and surrounding community … The majority cultures' view of Sumner's community did not define the contributions of Sumner … Sumner lived on top of the world and not the reverse."

- Jacqueline Anderson Batie '64: "No one just gave you grades—you had to work for them. Sumner prepared me to compete with any other student in college."

- Carolyn Sue Davis '67: "I enjoyed being with students like myself and having teachers that I could relate to as role models."

- Phyllis Diane Brown Tasby '70: "My kids did not experience an all black school, and they missed a unique experience of that time."

Theme 3: A collaborative relationship between the community and the school resulted in a unified front to promote and sustain a positive vision and a "we can" behavior. The success of Sumner can be directly traced to the unyielding support of parents, churches, and civic and business leaders who looked out for the well-being of the school and its students. Members of the neighborhood network were jokingly referred to as sentinels, who kept an eagle eye on everything that went on in the school and the neighborhood. In the mornings, some stood in their doorways, drinking their first cup of coffee, while others stood in their yards or boldly on street corners to make their presence known. They phoned each other as well as teachers and administrators to share concerns about issues that may result in negative consequences, to support school events, and to spread news about opportunities for students' continued development. The Parent Teacher Association (P.T.A.) served as the formal support body, but the entire community shouldered responsibility for the success of the school.

- Marian Singleton Jackson '34: "Sumner students achieved because parents, neighbors, school administrators, and faculty expected us to do our best… The participation of parents and other residents of KCK in securing equal facilities at both ends of town—northwest and northeast [contributed to the Sumner story]—when they raised money for the school, it was for the students—not to beautify the teachers' restroom!"

- Josephine Campbell Vandiver Boone '36: "The community wanted Sumner students to achieve."

- Marcelyn Hutton Gilbert '52: "It takes a village!"

- Joanne M. Collins '53: "I have a responsibility to give back to my community and the world at large."

- Johnnie M. Wooten '58: "Staff, parental support, and the community were the strongest forces that kept Sumner together… The students, staff, parents, and the community worked together."

- Carl Johnson '61: "We were a community (neighborhood) of people who really cared about each other."

- J. Clifford Oliver '61: "Community support and continued interest in school affairs and sports by former students [contributed to the Sumner story]. Sumner was a community institution."

- Beverly Reed Mister '64: "I never realized or understood the value of the educational system I was in… while I was in it. Probably because I had nothing to compare it to. All my life, an all black community was all I knew (doctors, dentists, churches, etc.) except for going shopping… I have tried to get my kids to understand the value of what we had, both in the school system and the community, but I don't think they've ever gotten it. They've never lived in an all black community like I grew up in."

- David R. Jones '64: "In our community, we could be what we wanted to be, and I felt very good about that feeling. It was a closed community, because we all lived in the northeast section of the city (doctors, lawyers and Indian chiefs). Your status played a part in the community; however, your status did not dictate you living in an exclusive neighborhood."

- Bernard Herschel Batie '65: I would choose to be educated at Sumner because of, "The love of the community and those who went before me, mother, father, sister, uncles, aunts, grandmother, and all the neighbors in the northeast area of KCK. Everybody loved Sumner."

- Beverly Rice Harris '65: "A sense of belonging and acceptance… enveloped the total school community."

- Franklin Preston '65: "Community took pride in seeing that a Sumnerite did well."

IDENTIFYING A CENTRAL MESSAGE

This chapter captures some of the varied impressions from five generations of Sumner alumni. Despite the range of recollections, a central message surfaces. Sumner's very foundation was based on one guiding principle: a good education is serious business. It's not "nice" to have; it's imperative. It is the preparatory system that opens the doors to the American promise of life, liberty, and the pursuit of happiness. It is the delivery system for navigating and negotiating the world. What happened at Sumner had a far-reaching impact; students remembered the people, behaviors, dispositions, events, and experiences of times past. Their memories brought texture to their lives; they helped shape their understanding of who they are and the roles they currently play.

What happened at Sumner was not happenstance. The astute and caring principals and teachers went to great lengths to make sure that students had a wide array of exposure and rigorous preparation. They knew that what they provided would ultimately serve as tools and resources for students to meet future challenges of advanced study, work, and family life. The message they collectively imparted to Sumnerians was that hard and consistent work merited rewards. Compromising for mediocrity and accepting less than full potential of self and others were not desirable. They taught students that the community—the people, churches, businesses, and civic organizations—was important and that individuals must give back to ensure their community's continued survival. Sumner taught that respect for others was premised on self-respect. For these lessons, Sumner's serious commitment to the business of education will live into perpetuity.

Graduates of Sumner are charged to ensure that the spirit of urgency, humanity, and tenacity to obtain a quality education is passed on to their descendants. Spartans must exemplify the benefits of good schooling. They must celebrate what happened in the past but can't rest on the laurels of what Sumner was. Alumni must claim responsibility and accountability for passing the baton of reality that a good education is serious business. They must think, say, and do those things that will, in years to come, be sources of strength as well as reservoirs of fond memories for their progeny.

CHAPTER SIX
FRUIT YIELDED

·······································

My Sumner experience prepared me to meet the challenges of life as a first-class rather than a second-class citizen, despite the status quo.

— Bonnie Collins Frazier, Class of 1964

High standards, a steeled focus on academic achievement, and unrelenting but supportive teachers provided a strong frame for preparing students to negotiate the world beyond Sumner. School documents and self-reported data reveal that, dating back to its very beginnings, a significant number of alumni, both male and female, from each decade earned college degrees. That Sumner was the only high school blacks in Kansas City, Kansas, could attend for more than half of its history, undoubtedly explains the large numbers of black students attending colleges from Kansas coming from one primary institution for decades. However, that the faculty was highly educated and served as role models or "proof positive" that obtaining advanced training was not only desirable but also highly feasible, fueled the desires and dreams of prospective collegians. In great measure, teachers' confidence in and encouragement of their students were undeniable factors impacting the flood of post–high school achievements.

Unlike the alarming number of college freshmen today who are awakened abruptly by the reality of their poor academic preparation, Sumner graduates found themselves well equipped for their continued academic pursuits. They took to heart the constant reminder to not only "be the best," but to be "twice as good" as everyone outside of the race. The high frequency of success experienced by Sumner graduates and their offspring, as evidenced by degrees, licenses, and certifications earned and other personal and professional accomplishments, speak definitively to the influence of this exceptional school. Students leaving the doors of Sumner excelled in art, business, the clergy, education, entertainment, law, literature, medicine, military, music, politics, and science.

The "mini-bios" and listings captured in this chapter reveal only a small fraction of the post-Sumner victories for thousands of its graduates. They serve as prelude to a self-perpetuating legacy of an outstanding educational experience. These abbreviated chronicles illustrate the tremendous effect that a school can have on the lives of its students long after they leave its doors. In decades to come, it is the expectation that the Sumner story will continue to live and grow through its graduates and their progeny. It is the challenge of the reader whose education is rooted in Sumner to rewrite this chapter continuously and to add as many names and as much information about the beneficiaries of the Sumner experience as can be found.

FIRST FRUITS

Not only will Sumner High School and the athletic field, which was authorized under the National Historic Preservation Act of 1966, go down in history as a place of significance, more important, its raisons d'être—its graduates—have claimed their places in local and national annals as well. Whether based on gender, ethnicity, or the nature of their accomplishments, the following list represents a small glimpse into some of the Spartans' post–high school pursuits. The individuals who opened doors are important, however, the influence of the collective body of graduates whose influence spans the globe is the real cause for celebration in this story.

Figure 6.1 A Few "Firsts" by Sumner Alumni

- Banks, Lacy '61—first black reporter for the Kansas City Star

- Blackmon Love, Johnnieque '63—first black school media specialist in Jefferson County Public Schools of Colorado; first diversity librarian at the University of Kansas

- Boone Fisher, Linda '65—first person to receive the Josephine Nevins Keal Fellowship at the University of Michigan for outstanding contributions to microbiology

- Booth Eason, Lillian '39—first black, first woman to serve as manager in Kansas City, Kansas, Office of Social Security 1942–1981

- Bowie, Walter C. '43—established first comparative cardiovascular laboratory in the United States; Established first heart-lung bypass machine for horses

- Caruthers, Sr., Bertram '29—first black principal of Hawthorne Elementary School in Kansas City, Kansas (Hawthorne was renamed Bertram Caruthers, Sr. Elementary School in 2002)

- Caruthers, Patricia W. '57—first black female instructor at Kansas City, Kansas Community College in 1969; first black female administrator at Kansas City, Kansas Community College in 1972; first black female to earn the Doctor of Philosophy Degree in Education at the University of Missouri at Kansas City in 1975; first black female member of Kansas Board of Regents

- Cates, Margie '48—first black female to graduate from Kansas University Medical School

- Evans, Dorsey '52—first black president of the Young Democrats in Washington, D.C.

- Foster, William P. '41—first recipient of the United States Achievement Academy Hall of Fame Award from the School of Education of the University of Kansas Alumni Association

- Franklin, Wallace J. '57—first black administrator in Shawnee Mission School District

- Freelain Bonner, Wilma '64—first black female principal of Wilson High School in Washington, D.C.

- Gaitan, Fernanado J. '67—first black and youngest judge appointed to the Appellate Bench in Kansas City, Missouri Western District, 1986

- Givens, Hoyt '44—first black to take the football field at Owen Stadium in Norman, Oklahoma, playing for Kansas State University in 1950

- Hall, Gerald '50—first black elected president of the Kansas City, Kansas Board of Education; first black chairman of Kansas City, Kansas Community College; first African- American chairman of the KCK Port Authority

- Holbert, Joanne '60—first black and first female deputy mayor of Pontiac, Michigan

- Hopkins, Lea '62—first black Kansas City, Kansas, Playboy Bunny (fourth black Bunny in the nation); first black professional Barbizon model in Kansas City; first black assistant director at the Metropolitan Museum of Art in New York City; cofounder of Christopher Street Association

- Hunter, Harold '44: first black to sign a contract with the National Basketball Association in 1950; first black to coach the U.S. Olympic basketball team

- Jackson, Elmer Jr. '29—first black member of the Kansas Board of Regents

- Jackson, William '46—first black professional employee of New Mexico State University

- Jenkins, Melvin E. '40—first recipient of unsolicited research grant from the National Institutes of Health (NIH) to the Department of Pediatrics at Howard University in 1958

- Jewell Jarett, Willie '54—first to locate minority-owned business in the Indian Springs Shipping Center (The Rib Shack)

- Jones, Minnie "Suma" '56—first black barber instructor at Raffler's Hair Design College

- Justice, Norman '52—first black man to reach rank of sergeant with Kansas City, Kansas Police Department

- Lewis, Delano '56—first black president and chief executive officer of the National Public Radio Network

- McClendon, John, Jr. '32—first coach to win three consecutive national titles at HBCU; first black to coach the National All-Star Team; first black coach in the American Basketball Association with the Denver Rockets; first black coach on the Olympic coaching staff; first black coach in the National Industrial Basketball League; first black coach to win the National AAU championship; first black coach to author book on basketball, Fast Break Basketball Fine Points and Fundamentals

- Meeks, Cordell D. '30—first black Democratic District Court judge of Kansas

- Monday, Veda '66—first black woman elected to Kansas City, Kansas Council under the mayor/council form of government

- Owens, Chester, Jr. '49—first black city official on Kansas City, Kansas Council

- Poole, Kenneth Lewis '50—first black deputy fire chief of the Kansas City, Kansas Fire Department

- Rice Harris, Beverly '65—first black female assistant chief probation officer for the Alameda County Probation Department

- Strickland Pinkard, Delores '62—first black elected internationally to Kansas University's National Alumni Association

- Sykes, Don '56-first African-American elected as vice president of United Airlines: vice president of Central Division Ground Operations

- Taylor, Henry '67—first black new car dealership owner in northwestern section of the country, Washington State, Oregon

- Tiller, Mary '55—first African-American TWA flight attendant

- Titus, Myer '50—first black administrator of Longview Community College of Metropolitan Junior College of Kansas City, Missouri, 1974

- Waters, Robert H. '44—first black professor at the Miami University Law School

- Weems, Christine '48—first black to graduate from the University of Kansas School of Nursing at the University of Kansas, 1953

- Young, John E. '64—first black tenure-track professor at the University of Denver School of Business at Boulder; first black to receive tenure at the University of Colorado School of Business at Denver; first black to receive tenure at the School of Management at the University of New Mexico

LEGAL EAGLES, MEDICAL MARVELS, AND SO MUCH MORE

There are so many Sumner graduates who soared and are still flying high in the fields of art, business, the clergy, education, law, medicine, and science. "The Story of Sumner High School Kansas City, Kansas," commissioned by beloved English teacher Ms. Scottie P. Davis, chronicled the names of 143 alumni who graduated prior to 1935 and earned undergraduate and/or graduate degrees. They began taking their places in the professional world in an era when careers were limited and opportunities were sparse, but they persevered (see figure 6.2). But the story of Sumnerites who applied skills, attitudes, and knowledge that were securely anchored in Sumner High School is rich. The few hundred post-'35 graduates who are highlighted or listed in the remainder of this chapter only scratch the surface of the fruit yielded from the fertile educational orchard of Sumner.

Figure 6.2 Degrees Earned by Sumner Graduates by 1935

Abernathy, Aulette	A.B.	University of Kansas
Austin, Ewell	B.S.	University of Chicago
Barksdale, Helen	B.S.	Kansas State Teachers College, Emporia
Bills, Samuel	A.B.	University of Kansas
Boggess, Dale	A.B.	Howard University
Bradley, Franklin	LL.B.	University of Kansas
Brister, Isaac	A.B.	University of Kansas
Brown, Harry	B.S.	University of Kansas
Browne, Albert	B.D.	Wilberforce University
Browne, Howard	LL.B.	Howard University
Browne, Hugh	M.D.	Howard University
Burdette, Sylvia	A.B.	University of Kansas
Burdix, Freddie	A.B.	University of Kansas
Burgin, Lillilan	A.B.	University of Kansas
Carroll, Matthew	A.B.	University of Kansas
Caruthers, Bertram	A.B.	University of Kansas
Caruthers, Percy	A.B.	University of Kansas
Claughton, Katherine	B.S.	Ohio State College
Clendennon, Claude	A.B.	University of Kansas
Clinch, Vernie	A.B.	University of Kansas
Cole, Simon	B.S.	University of Kansas
Collins, Joseph	B.S.	Kansas State Teachers College, Emporia
Cooper, James	Ph.G.	University of Kansas
Cotton, Robert	B.S.	Hampton Institute
Crump, Oliver	A.B.	Morehouse College
Davis, James	LL.B.	University of Kansas
Davis, William T. III	A.B.	Ohio University
Dickson, Catherine	A.B.	University of Kansas
Dwiggins, Horace	A.B.	University of Kansas
Emery, Ellurena	B.S.	Kansas State Agriculture College, Manhattan
Freeman, George	B.S.	Orangeburg State School, S.C.
Freeman, James	B.S.	Hampton Institute

French, DeKoven	M.D.	Howard University
French, Shelton	Ph.G.	Meharry Medical College
French, Wendell	Ph.G.	Meharry Medical College
Gatewood, Alexander	B.M.	University of Kansas
Green, Thomas	LL.B.	Washburn College
Greene, Frank	B.S.	Kansas State Agriculture College, Manhattan
Harlan, Mae	A.B.	University of Kansas
Hill, Kenneth	A.B.	Howard University
Hill, Letchen	A.B.	Howard University
House, Columbus	A.B.	University of Kansas
Howard, A.B.	LL.B.	Howard University
Howard, Madeline	B.S.	Kansas State Teachers College, Pittsburg
Howard, Romalee	A.B.	Ottawa College
Howell, Norman	D.V.M.	Kansas State Agriculture College, Manhattan
Jackson, Arlene	A.B.	University of Illinois
Jackson, Brydie	A.B.	University of Kansas
Jackson, Elmer	LL.B.	University of Kansas
Jackson, Mattie	B.S.	Kansas State Teachers College
Jackson, Nelson	A.B.	University of Minnesota
Jackson, Vera G.	A.B.	University of Kansas
James, Agnes	B.S.	Kansas State Teachers College, Emporia
Jenkins, Yvette	A.B.	University of Kansas
Johnson, Elnora	A.B.	University of Kansas
Jones, Evelyn	B.S.	University of Kansas
Jones, Herman	A.B.	University of Kansas
Jones, Oscar	B.S.	Hampton Institute
Jordan, Robert	A.B.	University of Kansas
Juanita Washington	A.B.	University of Kansas
Kealing, Hightower	A.B.	Lincoln University
Lane, Florence	A.B.	University of Kansas
Lannagan, Clyde	A.B.	University of Iowa
Lewis, Edward	A.B.	University of Chicago
Lewis, Joseph	DD.S.	Howard University
Link, Mary	A.B.	University of Chicago
Maddox, Albert	M.D.	Howard University
Maddux, Walter	A.B.	University of Kansas
Mansfield, Rostell	A.B.	Morehouse College
Matthews, Dan	A.B.	University of Kansas

Mobiley, Cornelius	D.V.M.	Kansas State Agriculture College, Manhattan
Mobiley, Paul	A.B.	University of Kansas
Monroe, Milton	D.V.M.	Kansas State Agriculture College, Manhattan
Nicholas, Gerren	B.M.	University of Kansas
Nicholson, Cecil	B.S.	Howard University
Orme, Beltram	A.B.	University of Kansas
Orme, Evelyn	A.B.	University of Kansas
Oscar, Eula	A.B.	University of Kansas
Parker, Freddie	B.S.	Kansas State Agriculture College, Manhattan
Payne, Cozetta	A.B.	Howard University
Payne, Ransom	DD.S.	Meharry Medical College
Pinkard, Wilbur	M.D.	University of Kansas
Radford, Arthur	M.D.	Meharry Medical College
Roan, Mattie	A.B.	Howard University
Robbins, Harold	B.S.	Hampton Institute
Ross, Alberta	A.B.	University of Kansas
Ross, Marie	B.M.	University of Kansas
Scales, Olivia	A.B.	University of Kansas
Scott, Naomi	A.B.	Lincoln University
Shelton, Willard	A.B.	University of Kansas
Simpson, Elizabeth	B.S.	Kansas State Teachers College, Emporia
Smith, Eleanor	B.S.	Hampton Institute
Smith, Margaret	B.S.	Fisk University
Smith, Willard	A.B.	University of Kansas
Terrell, Levi	B.D.	Morehouse College
Thatcher, Harold	B.S.	University of Minnesota
Thatcher, James	B.S.	Hampton Institute
Thomas, Earl	A.B.	University of Chicago
Thomas, J. Harrison	B.S.	University of Kansas
Thompson, Douglass	A.B.	University of Minnesota
Thompson, Louise	A.B.	University of Kansas
Thompson, Solomon	B.S.	Hampton Institute
Thurston, Thelma	A.B.	University of Minnesota
Tillman, Richard	A.B.	University of Kansas
Towers, Willie	LL.B.	University of Kansas
Turner, Zatella	A.B.	University of Kansas
Ward, Wayman	A.B.	Universityof Denver
Washington, Juanita	A.B.	University of Kansas

White, Helen	A.B.	University of Kansas
Wilkerson, Doxey	A.B.	University of Kansas
Wilkerson, Vernon	A.B.	University of Kansas
Williams, John	Ph.G.	Kansas State Teachers College, Pittsburg
Williams, Theodore	D.V.M.	Kansas State Agriculture College, Manhattan
Wilson, John	M.D.	Meharry Medical College
Young, Russell	B.S.	Kansas State Agriculture College, Manhattan
Young, Valleda	B.S.	Kansas State Agriculture College, Manhattan

A METAPHOR

The 1961–1962 Sumner varsity basketball team was an outstanding collection of soon-to-be professionals in such areas as business, medicine and education. This team could have been any of a number of Sumner teams or co-curricular organizations between 1905 and 1978. But, because one of *The Sumner Story* writers was a member of this particular team and gave endless firsthand accounts of its experiences, this team was chosen as a metaphor to represent Sumner alumni. Who could have projected such a victorious future for those Spartans while watching them compete so valiantly but hopelessly for the regional championship? Though they were skilled at all the fundamentals of basketball,, they were blatantly and prejudicially refereed to defeat. Who would have guessed that they would become the true champions, after all? Among those who fought hard that night were: Bertram Caruthers '62 (physician—dermatologist), John Collins '62 (Kansas City Power & Light Company employee), Richard Dumas '62 (professional basketball player in the ABA, schoolteacher), Aldophus C. Favors '62 (pharmacist, physician—internal medicine, oncology), McArthur Hall '63 (high school administrator), William Owens '62 (accountant), Kenneth Cloud '63 (school teacher), William Starks '62 (Colorado state administrator), Herman Watson '62 (physician—surgeon), Eurvin Williams '62 (Department of Agriculture, Grain Division, thirty-seven-year employee), Dwight Henderson '63 (attorney), and Terrell Jackson '63 (Colgate Palmolive Company, thirty-five-year employee). They lost the game that night; they didn't qualify for the state tournament. However, this team, which touted a 19–2 record, serves as a micro-picture for the composite student body of Sumner. It exemplified a conglomeration of dynamic human potential trained and nurtured in a segregated, under-resourced school that was the brunt of a white-dominated community. Despite the outside prejudice, unfair practices, and discouragement, the character, stamina, vision, skills and integrity that were developed on the basketball court, in the classrooms, in the choir room, in the cafeteria, and throughout the school comprised the foundation upon which generations of thinkers and leaders were built at Sumner.

LAW

Representing graduates who made contributions in the field of law are sketches taken from the lives of Cordell Meeks Sr. '30, Cordell Meeks Jr. '60, George Cole '48, Dorsey Evans '48, Donald Hopkins '54, Delano Lewis '56, and Reginald McKamie '71.

Cordell Meeks Sr. '30, and his son, *Cordell Meeks Jr. '60,* were among the most revered attorneys in Kansas City, Kansas. Both were graduates of Sumner, both were graduates of Kansas University Law School, both served as Wyandotte County District Court judges, and both made significant impacts on the quality of life in Kansas City, Kansas. Judge Meeks Sr. was the first black democratic district judge in the state of Kansas and the first black in the state to be elected to a countywide office. He was one of the founders of the first black bank in Kansas, the Douglass State Bank. In the capacities of director, vice president, and vice chairman, he provided vision and oversight of the institution, which became the anchor for thousands of families as they made financial investments in homes, businesses, and personal portfolios. Like his father, Judge Meeks Jr. was steeped in the fight for equality and justice. He served as an officer and member on numerous boards, committees, and associations including, president of the Kansas Municipal Court Judges Association, chairman of the KU Alumni Association Board of Directors, KU Advisory Board for Minority Development, president of the Law Society Board of Governors, and the Community Development Advisory Board for the Juniper Gardens Children's Project. In 2001, the KU School of Law honored Judge Meeks Jr. with its Distinguished Alumnus Citation, which is the highest honor given by the university and the Alumni Association for service to humanity. In a separate gesture of appreciation and respect, the health clinic located at 4313 State in Kansas City, Kansas, has been named in his honor: Children's Mercy West The Cordell Meeks Jr. Clinic.

George Cole '48 was one of the Sumnerians who started college after graduation but was called to serve the country in war; his was the Korean War. He made a long but steady climb to reach his career goal, demonstrating the perseverance espoused so fervently and frequently at Sumner. On returning from his military duties, Cole enrolled at Northwestern University to pursue a degree in chemistry and accounting, which he attained in 1968. Determined to reach his life goal of becoming a lawyer, George worked during the day and studied law in the evening. In 1974, he earned the juris doctor degree from DePaul University and opened his first law office in Cottage Grove Chicago. In 1988, Cole was recognized for his stellar work and was appointed associate judge in the Circuit Court of Cook County. Judge Cole worked in many areas of the law but found his niche in probate court. He retired from the bench in 2000.

It was not his first chair trumpet status at Kansas University but, rather, his role in representing the guard who discovered the Watergate break-in that infamous night in 1972 that catapulted *Dorsey Evans '48* into national focus. He was the attorney for Frank Wills, the guard who was on duty the night burglars hired by the Committee to Reelect the President broke into the Democratic National Headquarters in Washington, D.C. Wills' actions and subsequent testimony led to the swift arrest of the five burglars and the ultimate impeachment of U.S. President, Richard M. Nixon. A graduate of Kansas University and Howard University Law School in 1958, Dorsey Evans successfully practiced law in the District of Columbia for more than fifty years. Attorney Evans played other strategic roles in the nation's capital, including, counsel for the Economic Development Division of PRIDE, Inc., cofounded by Marion Barry; legal counsel for the Howard University Student Loan Department; staff attorney for the Legal Aid Society of Washington, D.C.; and treasurer for Congressman Walter Fauntroy for the duration of his terms on the Hill, 1971 to 1990. Evans was also a certified real estate, financial, and mortgage broker. He served on numerous boards, including the District Cable Vision Board—Comcast, and contributed articles to the *Michigan Park Newspaper*.

Another Spartan who became an attorney, *Donald Hopkins '54*, confessed that he was bored at Sumner and disappointed that more of the latent talent was not developed. But Donald Hopkins also remembered the teachings of Mr. E. A. Taylor and Ms. Rebecca Bloodworth, whose efforts may have helped prepare him for the critical roles he played in his law career. After presiding over his junior and senior class at Sumner, Donald Hopkins distinguished himself early as a scholar. He was elected to Phi Beta Kappa at the University of Kansas during his senior year and eventually studied at some of the nation's most prestigious institutions, including Yale, the University of California at Berkeley, and Harvard. Hopkins received a law degree from the University of California, Berkeley School of Law and a master's degree from Harvard University Law School. While at Berkeley, Hopkins became the first African-American assistant to the dean of students (1965–1967); he also served as assistant executive chancellor for one year but then decided to pursue further studies in law at Harvard.

Attorney Hopkins joined the legal staff of the NAACP Legal Defense Fund but returned to California to become vice president of a management consultant firm. Notwithstanding his many accomplishments, Don Hopkins is nationally recognized for his strategic work as the district administrator for Representative Ron Dellums (1971–1992), who fought for civil and human rights throughout his twenty-seven consecutive years in Congress. Hopkins has traveled extensively in the Caribbean and has demonstrated his knowledge and understanding of the evolution of Cuba. As a prolific writer, Attorney Hopkins has contributed magazine articles to a number of publications, including the *Negro Digest* and *Ebony*.

"The teachers at Sumner High School had great influence on my life and great influence on many of the other students in Kansas City, Kansas. We had role models who had advanced degrees. We had role models who believed that blacks could learn, and they spent every ounce of energy to make sure that we succeeded...I had many role models, one being Solomon Henry Thompson Jr., who was the principal of Sumner High School. He was an incredible man, who believed that we were going to have a quality high school. He stressed discipline and academic excellence. Other role models included Robert Clarke, my band teacher; William Boone, chemistry; Rebecca Bloodworth, English; Rostelle Mansfield, science; and Bertram Caruthers, science... These men and women in education instilled confidence in many of us at Sumner." Crediting much of his success to his high school experiences, *Delano Lewis '56* garnered respect for his works from across the world. After completing undergraduate work at the University of Kansas, Delano earned his juris doctor degree from Washburn University School of Law and began an impressive career. His most noteworthy positions and assignments included associate director and country director for the Peace Corps in Nigeria and Uganda; president of the Chesapeake & Potomac Telephone Company; president and CEO of the National Public Radio, and U.S. ambassador to South Africa. One of his sons, Phil Lewis, has achieved national recognition for his stardom as Mr. Moseby in the television situation comedy, *The Suite Life of Zack and Cody*.

Attorney *Reginald E. McKamie '71* has a unique and prestigious background in the U.S. Merchant Marines. He was appointed captain in the U.S. Navy by President Bill Clinton and served as captain of several merchant marine ships, including S/S *Exxon Benicia* and S/S *Exxon North Slope*. Captain McKamie is a member of the U.S. Navigation Safety Advisory Council and a board member of the National Academy of Science Transportation Research Board in Washington, D.C. Specializing in maritime operations, his counsel is widely sought by seamen and their families, who have experienced injuries and damages while working offshore.

McKamie received his B.S. degree from the U.S. Merchant Marine Academy, Kings Point, New York, in 1975; an M.B.A. degree from the University of Southern California in 1976; and a J.D. degree from the University of Houston in 1986. McKamie was an adjunct professor of Maritime Law at Texas Southern University's Thurgood Marshall School of Law. Having attained proctor status, the highest membership rank lawyers receive in the Maritime Law Association of the United States, he is recognized and pursued nationally and internationally for his expertise in maritime law.

A few other Sumnerians who forged the field of law include Isaac J. Bradley '12, Riley Smith '18, William Towers '14, Elmer C. Jackson Jr. '29, Robert H. Waters '43 (James Weldon Johnson/Robert H. Waters Summer Institute and Robert H. Waters Black Law Students Association at the University of Miami School of Law were named in his honor), Donald Perkins '47, Donald Gayden '49, Judge Thomas McLaurin Jr. '60, Dwight Henderson '63, Waymon Favors '64, Judge Fernando Gaitan '67, Gregory King '66, Vernon Lewis '66, Jacques Barber '68, Aisha Gail McDaniel '73, Rosie Quinn '73, Peggy Abernathy '77 (court administrator) and Isaac Marks '77.

MEDICINE

Representing Spartans who labored in homes, hospitals, medical centers, and other venues that required healing hands are Vernon Wilkerson '17, Romelee Howard '30, Melvin Jenkins '40, Oneita Taylor Baker '64, and Michael Foggs '68.

Among some of the earliest graduates who became physicians was *Vernon Wilkerson, '17*. Although remaining in the Midwest to receive his training, the majority of Dr. Wilkerson's professional career was spent on the East Coast. As recorded in the "The Story of Sumner High School Kansas City, Kansas" (Davis, 1935), Vernon received his bachelor's and doctor of medicine degrees from the University of Kansas and the University of Iowa, respectively. He continued his studies at the University of Minnesota, receiving a Ph.D. in biochemistry with a minor in physiology. Dr. Wilkerson, who for a short period served as a house surgeon at General Hospital in Kansas City, became a valued member of the Howard University Medical School.

After graduating from Sumner in 1930, *Romelee A. Howard* studied chemistry at Ottawa University. In a conversation at the 2000 Sumner Conference, he revealed that he was the only black student in his class there. After earning his master's degree at Ottawa, he pursued the study of medicine at Howard University and graduated tenth in the Class of 1940. Dr. Howard chose to work for the U.S. Public Health Service and became involved in a study of venereal disease in Nashville, Tennessee, and Birmingham, Alabama. Later, he was sent to Florida to immunize migrant workers. Dr. Howard was also detailed to Monrovia, Liberia. He finished his career in private practice in the Bronx, New York. Of special note are the four children Dr. Howard and his wife raised: three became lawyers, and one became a medical doctor.

Another Sumnerian to pursue medicine and make tremendous inroads in health was *Melvin E. Jenkins Jr. '40*. "As the only black high school in the state of Kansas, it was highly competitive academically. Not only did we dominate in Westinghouse Science Fairs … we excelled in other venues." Dr. Jenkins received his medical degree from the University of Kansas. He continued his studies at Freedmen's Hospital in Washington, D.C., with a special focus on sickle cell pathophysiology, and at Johns Hopkins Hospital in the area of pediatric endocrinology. Dr. Jenkins became a full-time faculty member in the Department of Pediatrics at Howard University in 1958. As such, he received a research grant from the National Institutes of Health (NIH) to investigate fetal hemoglobin in maternal circulation. In 1961, while studying with Dr. Frederick C. Bartter of NIH, his patient was the first in the world to have been reported with the Bartter's Syndrome. In 1969, Dr. Jenkins was appointed professor of pediatrics at the University of Nebraska, where he developed the academic, research, and clinical components of Nebraska's first program in pediatric endocrinology. However, he returned to Washington, D.C., in 1973 and chaired the Howard University Department of Pediatric and

Child Health until 1986. He also served on the faculties of George Washington University and Johns Hopkins University.

Dr. Jenkins served on numerous national committees, task forces, and study sections at the U.S. Public Health Service, the Department of Agriculture, the American Academy of Pediatrics, and the National Institutes of Health. He was instrumental in the development of the Nutrition Metabolic Laboratory at Ile-Ife, Nigeria. He served as a consultant and lecturer at health facilities in six continents and the Caribbean.

Dr. Oneita Taylor '64 is a highly regarded radiation oncologist at the Cancer Treatment Centers of America Southwestern Cancer Hospital. Dr. Taylor, who was honored with the Outstanding Achievement Award by the 1994 Consortium of Female Physicians, is certified by the American Board of Radiology in Therapeutic Radiology and is a diplomate of the National Board of Medical Examiners. She has expertise in the treatment of colon cancer and early stages of breast cancer and has presented lectures on these topics at major medical conferences. Dr. Taylor's publications include "Local Recurrence in Rectosigmoid Colon After Curative Surgical Resection," which appeared in the *Journal of the National Medical Association*. Dr. Taylor received her medical degree from Kansas University and completed her residency in radiation oncology at the University of Kansas Medical Center. She worked for almost ten years as a chemist for the U.S. Department of Agriculture in Kansas City, Kansas, and was owner of the Tulsa X-Ray Laboratories, Inc., in Tulsa, Oklahoma.

Michael Foggs '68 is recognized for his extensive work in allergy and immunology. After graduating from Sumner, he studied biology and cellular ultra structure at Yale University, where he received his bachelor's of science degree. Dr. Foggs earned his medical degree from Harvard Medical School and completed his internship and residency in internal medicine at Northwestern University. As the chief of Allergy, Asthma, and Immunology at Chicago's Asthma Health Centers, Dr. Foggs has stressed the reality of blacks and Puerto Ricans having the highest frequencies of asthma and that control of the condition is the goal.

Dr. Foggs's professional roles include, associate director of Allergy and Immunology at Hahnemann University Medical Center and School of Medicine in Philadelphia, Pennsylvania; immediate past chairman of the Allergy, Asthma and Immunology Section of the National Medical Association (NMA); chairman of the Managed Care & Health Plans Committee of the American College of Allergy, Asthma, & Immunology (ACAAI); fellow of the American Academy of Allergy, Asthma & Immunology, and the American College of Allergy, Asthma, & Immunology, and the American College of Chest Physicians.

Other Spartans who became physicians include: John Wilson '07, Arthur Bradford '10, Harold Thatcher '25, Hamilton Perkins '27, Wallace Dooley '38, Jessie Spearman '39, Andrew Henderson '56, BertramCaruthers '62, Adolphus C. Favors '62, Juanita Washington '62, Herman Watson '62, and Marvin McIntosh '68.

Other medical fields Spartans pursued included nursing: Alversia Jackson Eaton '26, Georgia Jackson Ferguson '32, Margaret Washington Cooper (LPN) '33, Naomi Scott (aide) '35, Bethene Freelain King '36, Dorothy Henderson Peters '36, Lodene Herron Hoover '39, Ada Coffey Williams '49, Norma Porter Currie '44, Learline Newman Mason '45, Mamie Richardson '47, Marialice Davis Everett (LPN) '48, Claudia Herron Orr '48, Christine Weems Northern '48, Betty Ward Taliaferro '49, Patty Irene Carter '50, Smith McManus '50, Alice Ward Russell '50, , Shirley Webster Howard (LPN) '52, Faye Ward Fenwick '52, Alma Thompson Henson (LPN) '53, Sylvia Thierry Sykes '54, Teola Chandler Tilman '55, Rosa Hess Bagsby (LPN) '57, Marie Williams Morris '57, Lavera Clay Mitchem '62, Wanda Berry Redeemer '65, Juanita Carr '65, Betty Dean Jones '65, Brenda Early '65, Renee Randolph Ellis '65, Beverly Johnson King '65, Barbara Madlock '65, Betty Williams VanRoss '65, Charlotte Johnson Webb '69, Adrienne Williams '77

Medical technologists included: Margie Harrison '47, Suzanne Thompson Knowles '49, and Dorothy Watson McField '53. Some pharmacists include: James Strickland '47 and Adolphus C. Favors '62. Physical therapists were: Henry Thompson '47, Barbara White '51, and Rudolph Morris '53. Janice Jarrett '78 was among the optometrists. Dentists include: Howard Dodd '53, Thomas Jones '58, Freddie Bailey '64, and Evelyn Burton '65. Radiologists include: Sylvia Smith '47 and Ethel Fairley Moore '52. Arlene Johnson Jones '56 is counted with the phlebotomists. Some veterinarians were: Theodore S. Williams '31 (Tuskegee University School of Veterinary Medicine is named in his honor), and Walter C. Bowie '43.

Among the registered dieticians who kept bodies healthy through good nutrition were: Jeanne Patterson Harper '43, Edith Armstrong Green '56, Sandra Freelain '63, and Charlotte Ferrell '64.

EDUCATION

Education was one of the early professional areas Sumner graduates pursued and populated impressively in both the Greater Kansas City Metropolitan Area and communities across the nation. Interest, skills, impressive role models, and ready access to positions in the field may have been determining influences. Among those Spartan educators were the principals of Northeast Junior High School, Joseph Collins and William H. Boone, and Solomon H. Thompson, the second-longest reigning principal of Sumner. Mr. Collins started his career as a science teacher at Western University; he served as principal of Northeast Junior High School from 1933 to 1958. Mr. Boone began his career in education at Northeast Junior High School in the fall of 1947 as a science and mathematics teacher. From 1952 to 1958, he taught chemistry at Sumner. He served as principal of Northeast from 1958 to 1973. Mr. Thompson, who taught at Western University, Northeast Junior High School, and Sumner reigned as principal of Sumner from 1951 until 1972.

Abel B. Sykes '52 was yet another Sumnerian who followed the education trail. Immediately on graduating from Sumner, however, he enlisted in the U.S. Air Force. Right after training, he realized and relied on the utility and quality of his high school experiences to make the most of his military assignment. After all, he shared, Sumner left him with the confidence that he, "could do anything." Although Sykes' intents were centered on becoming a pilot, he was summarily relegated to serve in food services. His protests to the assignment were not acknowledged until he let it be known that he was a skilled musician and, furthermore, had been an excellent drum major (under the expert tutelage of none other than Mr. Robert N. Clark). Sykes had done his homework; he knew the unit's band was in need of his skills. Not surprisingly, Sykes leveraged his skills to become a vital member of the 35th Air Force Band in Sacramento, California. Several years later, when he was offered the opportunity to train for his original choice of pilot, he declined. He completed his stint in the military and later purchased his personal plane, as a civilian. The majority of Dr. Sykes' post–high school accomplishments are centered in higher education, not the military.

A graduate of Kansas City Junior College, University of Kansas City (now University of Missouri at Kansas City) and the University of California at Los Angeles, Dr. Sykes has served on the faculties of Grossmont College in El Cajon, California, and Michigan University. He has gained great esteem in the collegiate circles for his work as president of Compton Community College, president of King River Community College in Fresno, and president of Lansing Community College in Lansing, Michigan. Among his many other accomplishments, he was awarded the Fulbright Award to China in 1986 and dubbed the "Educator of the Year" from Phi Delta Kappa in 1972.

Known for her hard work and indefatigable spirit, *Dr. Delores Strickland Pinkard '62* has played a critical role in the school system of Kansas City, Kansas. In 1995, she culminated her career as vice president for executive services of the Kansas City, Kansas Community College. Prior to that, she served as a classroom teacher, principal, and director of elementary personnel of Kansas City, Kansas public schools.

After reflecting on the care and support provided to him at Sumner High School, *Dr. Myer Titus '50* admitted that he could not turn down the opportunity to do the same for students of Philander Smith College in Little Rock, Arkansas. From 1989 to 1999, he served as the president of this well-known, historically black college, his alma mater. A former minister of the neighborhood church (Mason Memorial) actually encouraged Titus to attend college after high school. "I had never been away from home, but I took him up on his offer for a working scholarship. I majored in sociology and minored in psychology. When I went to Sumner, I concentrated on building trades but found out that I actually had a tremendous background in math and science." Titus completed his undergraduate studies and went on to graduate school in the area of secondary education at the University of Arkansas at Fayetteville. He was drafted and sent to Korea with about nine hours of outstanding work to complete his master's degree. After returning from the army in 1957, Titus was hired at the Bendix Corporation in Kansas City as its first salaried black employee. There, he discovered a new area of expertise: computers. Dr. Titus received initial training at Bendix but eventually went on to get his doctorate degree in computer science from the University of Missouri at Columbia. While completing his advanced studies, Dr. Titus found his niche in the college environment. On his rise to Philader Smith, he served as associate dean of instruction at Metropolitan Junior College, vice president for instruction at Pikes Peak Community College in Colorado Springs, campus president at the Community College of Denver at Auraria, and associate vice president for the Colorado Community College System (all of the community colleges of the state). "I have spent a lot of time going to classes and different colleges, workshops, and seminars. Some of the best instruction that I have ever seen in my life was at Eighth and Oakland."

Some other Sumner alumni who left imprints at the university level include Desdemona West Davis '14—music at Texas Southern University; Mary Link '21 (Phi Beta Kappa)—dean of women at University of Chicago, Tuskegee University; J. Harrison Thomas '25—music at Florida A&M University; Zatella Turner (Phi Beta Kappa) '25—English at Virginia Union; Nicholas Gerren '30—music at Lincoln University, Texas Southern University, and Central State University; Thelma Thurston Gerham '31—journalism at Florida A&M; Louis Whitworth '36—chair of Music Department at Chicago State University; William Foster '37—music at Fort Valley State College and Florida A&M; Clestia Herron Fraction '37—counselor at Metropolitan Junior College; Charles Sherman '37—education at Illinois State University; Tyree Jones Miller '39—chair of English Department at Tennessee State University; Walter C. Bowie '43—chair of Department of Physiology and Pharmacology Department and dean of School of Veterinary Medicine at Tuskegee University; Richard Miller '44—kinesiology and coach at Tennessee State University; William Jackson '46—New Mexico State University; Otis Simmons '46—music at Philander Smith College, Texas Southern University, Southern University, and Alabama State University; Leroy Pitts '51—biology at Penn Valley Community College; Glenda Foggs Thompson '53—English at Milwaukee Area Technical College; Nathan T. Davis '55—music at University of Pittsburgh; Edward A. Eddy '56-dean of education at Rockhurst College, Chicago State University, North Park University, and Aurora University; Reginald Buckner '57—music at Kansas University; Patricia Caruthers '57—administrator at Kansas City, Kansas Community College; Maxine Smith Claire '57—English at George Washington University; Johnnie Ruth Ersery Thompson '60—African Studies at Wichita State University; Jo Anne Holbert '60—Wayne State University; Arthur Spears '61 (Phi Beta Kappa)—anthropology/linguistics, City University of New York; George Crump '62—Kansas City, Kansas Community College; dorether M. Welch '62—sociology at Penn Valley Community College; Brenda Williams Mercomes '62—administrator at Roxbury Community College; Johnnieque Blackmon Love '63—academic librarianship at University of Kansas, Texas A&M, University of Maryland; Edward Underwood '63- education at the University of Missouri at Kansas City; Wilma Freelain Bonner '64—education at Howard University; Earnestine Jones Harrison '64—

management and technology, Rio Salado College; John Young '64—business at University of Colorado School of Business at Boulder and at Denver, the School of Business at University of New Mexico; Linda Boone Fisher '65—chair, Microbiology Department at University of Michigan, Dearborn Campus; and Elizabeth Sparks '69—counseling at Boston College.

Some Sumner alumni who became educators (^ counselors, *administrators, consultants and teachers) on the PK–12 level include: Elgetha Allsbrook '10, Allye Cornell '10, Ersa Dorsey Brown '10, Sallie Brown '11, Gaynell Johnson, '11, May McClelland, '11, Lucy Neely '11, Jessica Neely '12, Lenora Russell '13, Minnie Tucker '13, Lillie Adams '14, Bertha Barner '14, Hazel Capps '14, Eulala Haynes '14, Myrtle Smith '14, Daisy Whitfield '14, Eva Grant '15, Eva Howell '15, Arlene C. Jackson '15, Lillie Mae Green '16, Corrine Lightbody '16, Supora Miller '16, Ella Smith '16, Hilda Graves '17, Leona Irvin '17, Nadine Stepp Watson '17, Glena Wright '17, Maude Allen '18, Hortense Flower '18, Ella Neely '18, Lela Plummer '18, Mattie Roan '18, Mildred Welton '18, Dale B. Bouggess '19, Flossie Cotton '19, Beatrice Anderson '21, James Thatcher '22, Christine Walton Thompson '22, Hester Jackson Murchison '23, *Christine Walton Thompson, *Marian Singleton Jackson '24, *Herman Theodric Jones '25 (Jones Intermediate School of Prairie View named in his honor), Wilma Leach Caverl '25, ^Mazie Walton Mitchell '26, Ella Mae Miles '27, Velma Orme Simpson '27, Rosetta Bivens Jackson '28, ^Bertram Caruthers '29, Irene Goldie Everett '29, *Lillian Taylor Orme '29, Barbara Mason '30, Hazel Blair Anderson '31, Bertie Everett Alsbrook '31, Evelyn Gerren Townsell '31, Evelyn Orme Caruthers '31, S. Grace Bailey '32, Gussia Addison Butler '34, *Irma Sisson Walker '34, ^Josephine Campbell Vandiver Boone '36, Arlene Orme Young '36, Celestia Herron Fraction '37, Lucy Bartee Sanders '39, *Linis Boswell '39, ^Arvestine Muzzle Williams '39, Verdaine Sanders Curry '39, Emma Jean Jones McIntosh '40, Irene Mahone George '41, ^Elizabeth Morgan Robinson '41, Johnella Newton '41, Mattie Smith McCluney '41, Anita Patterson Gray '42, Lillian Poole Hendricks '43, Frank Powell '43, Mary Jenkins Watkins '44, Mable Caldwell Lee '45, *William James Herron '45, ^Annabelle Bolden Knox '46, Shirley Border '46, Sarah Daugherty Carr '47, Eva Fine Bracey '47, ^Gladys Harrison McClain '47, Theodore Madison '47, Martha Morgan Eulinberg '48, Paulyne Patterson Depp '48, James Spicer '48, Barbara Curtis Dwight '50, *Charles Dwight '50, Paul B. Graham '50, Gerald Hall '50, Leroy Pitts '51, ^Hargest H. Shumate '51, Herbert Thompson '51, Beverly Jean

Scott '54, Marcelyn Hutton Gilber '54, Shirley Ross '54, Judith Walker Jackson '54, Gloria Franklin Watson '55, Harold Herron '55, LaLeta Schuler Jones '55, *Elaine Arnold '56, Sadie Blackmon-Cole '56, Eldora Chandler Gray '56, Norma Curtis Hickman '56, *Nyra Harris '56, Gwendolyn Jackson Horton '56, Betty Rice Gibson '56 (taught in Liberia West Africa for eleven years), Marilyn DeGraftenreed Thompson '57, Craig Hall '57, Bernadine Mason '57, Franklin Wallace '57, Sonia Thierry Holbert '57, Bernice Long Johnson '58, Barbara Rice Morris '58, Johnnie M. Wooten '58, Marva Hooks Hall '59, Carole Arnold Ellison '59, Karen Sears Vertreese '59, Sharon Thierry Buckner '59, Yvonne Anderson Howell '60, Walter Bailey '60, Sandra Batie Garrett '60, ^Donna Mitchell Plummer '60, *Louis Plummer '60, John Rice '60, Jacquelyn Brown Williams '61, Alice Yates Banks '61, Joanne Foggs Wilkerson '62, *Jessie Kirksey '62, Sigora Porter '62, *Valera Richmond Jefferson '62, Rose Thierry Sims '62, Eugene M. Williams '62, Johnnieque Blackmon Love '63, McArthur Hall '63, Yvonne Moore Crowe '63, Marjorie Newman Owens '63, *Jacqueline Anderson Batie '64, Veda Brady Sherman '64, Minnie Davis Givens '64, Sarah Echols Smith '64, *Wilma Freelain Bonner '64, *Diana Howard Kolen '64, ^Lee James '64, Beatrice Tennyson '64, *Rose Walker Bunton '64, Yvonne Welch '64, *Monetta Whitcomb Foster '62, Jacqueline Anderson '65, ^Melanie Bailey '65, Patricia Barnes Hopkins '65, Earl Blackmon '65, Alice Hicks Clark '65, *Gloria Brown Johnson '65, Brenette Chandler Gardner '65, Judy Hadley Dangerfield '65, Jacqueline Hill Stephenson '65, Paul Hill '65, Curtis Long '65, *Warren G. Mason '65, Carolyn Mitchell '65, Paulette Newman Hall '65, Robert Parker '65, Verona Plummer Hughes '65, Jean Porchia Moten '65, Lawrence Williams '65, Marilyn Winn Webb '65, Murline Wright Akers '65, Donna Easterwood Carroll '66, Dorothy Garrett '66, Brenda C. Jones '66 (Member of KCK Board of Education), Yvonne Parks Brooks '65, Janice Riden Wilson '65, Joan Rogers '66, Captola Taylor Harris '66, *Marsha Winn Self '66, Marjorie Brown Miller '67, Larry McIntosh '67, Linda Newman Murray '67, *Melanie Thierry Prince '67, ^Stephanie Thierry McIntosh '67, Carolyn Sue Davis '67, *Andrea Smith '69, Phylliss Brown Tasby '70, and ^Gayle Chandler Lee '72.

Supporting educators in efforts to develop students and their families to their greatest potential are social workers and juvenile counselors. Sumnerians included in these ranks are: Louise Thompson Clark '19, Rudolph Gordon '43, Ora Kemp Collins '43, Susan Turner Johnson '45, Virginia Ferguson Freeman '48, Bertha Northern Beatty '48, Susan Turner Johnson '45, Jane Dillard Williams '56, Patricia

Freelain Moore '58, Carolyn Buford Jones '52, Marcena Meeks Chandler '63, Bonnie Collins Frazier '64, Beverly Rice Harris '65, Mary Jo Stuart Hoard '65.

CLERGY

Oh Lord God, supreme creator and ruler of the multiverse, keeper and giver of all wisdom and knowledge, we thank thee for Sumner High School, all that it ever stood for and all that it ever did for us and others. It was there where You blessed us with caring, sharing teachers who taught with a passion for perfecting people. Oh may our tongues cleave to the roofs of our mouths before we ever forget Sumner. And bless us that we will live our lives in a way that will continue to bring glory and honor to that legendary learning institution. Amen.

— Reverend Lacy J. Banks, Class of 1961

Although religion was not a course formally offered at Sumner, the recognition of a Being far greater than oneself was part and parcel of the culture before reaching Spartan Town. Prior to the 1960s, when prayer was banned in schools, "church school" was built into the elementary school program. Students left their classrooms each week and walked to neighborhood churches to learn about Christianity. A number of alumni pursued the clergy. Included in that group are Donald D. Clark '44, Edward Foggs '52, and the Banks brothers—Lacy '61, Jimmie '61, and Ephthallia '65.

Like so many of his classmates, *Donald Clark* was drafted into the army in the late 1940s. Prior to being drafted, Clark studied at Warner Pacific Bible College in Portland, Oregon, where he later earned a bachelor of theology degree. After completing his tour of duty in the U.S. Army, Clark served as associate pastor and pastor of the Beech Street Church of God in Oregon. By 1960, Reverend Clark decided to return to the military and pursue both his studies and career in religion. He was promoted through the years and ultimately reached the rank of colonel. His extensive education includes a master of divinity degree from Western Evangelical Seminary (Oregon), a master's of science degree from Butler University (Indiana), and studies in clinical pastoral education from the National Mental Health Association. As a student of both Greek and the New Testament, Colonel Clark translated the entire New Testament from Greek to English.

Serving as a chaplain in the army for over twenty-six years, some of the positions he held were: chief of the Leadership Branch of the Adjutant General School in Indiana; Command Chaplain in Okinawa, Japan; Division Chaplain for the Seventh Infantry Division in Fort Ord, California; deputy director of plans, programs, and policies for the Office of the Chief of Chaplains at the Pentagon in Washington, D.C.; and staff chaplain at Fort Stewart, Georgia. He served on the Armed Forces Chaplains Board, the Army Chief of Chaplains Personnel Board, the Secretary of the Army's Conscientious Objectors Review Board, the Department of the Army Human Use Review Board, and the Quality of Life Board. Clark also served as the project manager for two research studies for the Army Chief of Chaplains Department of the Army pamphlet, "Religious Requirements and Practices of Certain Selected Groups: A Handbook Supplement for Chaplains," and the Department of the Army Study, "Social Aspects of Chaplain Ministry." Chaplain Clark's assignments took him to more than twenty-five countries including, Austria, Belgium, China, Egypt, England, France, Germany, Greece, Israel, Japan, Korea, Lebanon, Switzerland, Taiwan, and Vietnam.

It was the plea of *Dr. Edward L. Foggs '52*, as chairman of the National Association of Evangelicals (NAE), for his membership to reach out with "compassionate help" in the wake of the 9/11 tragedy in 2001. As the largest wing of organized Christianity in America, his petition was heard and embraced by millions. Dr. Foggs has dedicated his life to spreading the word of Jesus Christ; his mission, assisted by the many influential positions he has held, has impacted the quality of life for many. He has served as pastor of the Sherman Street Church of God in Anderson, Indiana; director of Urban Ministries of the Church of God; board member of Church Extension and Home Missions of the Church of God; and the general secretary of the Leadership Council of the Church of God. In varied capacities, Dr. Foggs has helped churches to administer effectively in urban settings, facilitated major fundraising efforts, led churches in extensive restructuring projects, integrated autonomous church structures to promote collaboration rather than competition, and worked tirelessly to ensure that the NAE was ethnically and gender inclusive. On his entry into the position of chairman of this auspicious body, Dr. Foggs committed himself to diversity, "The NAE has been too male, too white, and too aging." He has played a major role in planning and executing worldwide conferences to bring people together in such places as Germany, Kenya, Korea, England, Malaysia, and Australia.

Dr. Foggs received his bachelor's degree in social science and business from Ball State University. He continued graduate studies in theology at Anderson University School of Theology, Christian Theological Seminary in Indiana, and Princeton Theological Seminary in New Jersey. He is the recipient of the doctor of divinity from Anderson University and the doctor of humane letters from Warner Pacific College. When he reflected on his days at Sumner, he credited Ms. Scottie P. Davis and Ms. Rebecca Bloodworth for his ability to use the English language. "Our teachers really cared about us, genuinely cared, encouraged and supported us … Back in those days, I got attention at Sumner that I would not have gotten at an integrated school." Not unlike many Sumner alumni, all of his children (five) completed college and became creative and productive members of society.

One of the most divine stories regarding men of the cloth is that of the Banks brothers—*Lacy '61, Jimmie '61*, and *Ephthallia '65*. Multitalented, articulate, hard-working, and persistent in accomplishing their goals, all three brothers were well known and well liked during their Sumner years. Losing their mother shortly after relocating to Kansas City, Kansas, from Lyon, Mississippi, the brothers were raised by their father, who was also a minister. In their submission to the *Sumner High School Alumni Association Family History,* they noted the instruction of their father to, "'Stay with the Lord,'" if they wanted to reach their potential. All three were actively engaged in the total life of the school—student council, class offices, and programs that involved music and oratory. Their post–high school pursuits reflect their multiple gifts and obvious adherence to their father's counsel.

Reverend Lacy Banks was the "boy preacher," who captivated his schoolmates as well as congregants from the various churches in the community with his lively cadence from the pulpit and his melodic notes from the choir loft. Although he never gave up the ministry, Lacy attended Kansas University on graduation from high school and pursued French, Spanish, and psychology as "a" major. However, for almost forty years, Reverend Banks has been esteemed as a prolific columnist and sportswriter for the *Chicago Sun Times* and a reporter for *Ebony* magazine. Just as he multitasked at Sumner, Reverend Banks has continued to pursue his passion for spreading the Word. He has preached at scores of churches throughout Illinois.

Known for keeping his hand, head, and heart on the pulse of the community, *Reverend Jimmie Banks,* pastor of Strangers Rest Baptist Church, belongs to various organizations and serves on several boards including, the Black Community

Fund, the Providence-St. Johns Foundation, and the Board of Governors of the Urban League. He addresses issues ranging from the Kansas City, Kansas Board of Education's outsourcing of work contracts to the persistent challenges of providing care for the indigent in Wyandotte County and identifying fiscal resources for prospective and current college students. Whether in the sanctuary, the boardroom, or his office, Reverend Banks' expertise is working with people. For over three decades, he worked in human resource management at Allied Signal. He has also continued to develop his musical talents; in the fall of 2009, he produced a CD titled *Songs that Strengthen and Soothe.* Reverend Banks earned his undergraduate and graduate degrees from Central Missouri State University and completed his theological studies at Western Baptist Seminary.

A graduate of Donnelly College and Western Baptist Seminary, *Reverend Ephthallia Banks* is the pastor of Greystone Heights Baptist Church. Multitalented like his brothers, Reverend Banks was a cofounder of Black Contemporary Players. This group had its own playhouse in the sixties and seventies and performed quarterly productions of ethnic dramas. Reverend Banks has continued to write plays and perform one-man shows with drama and songs for schools, churches, and social organizations. He is the director of transportation for the Unified Government of Wyandotte County.

Other Sumner graduates who answered a "higher calling" include: William Freelain '27, Charles B. Bailey '41, Raymond C. Higgs '41, Maynard T. Preston '41, Curtis Herron '49, William Lawson '52, Walter Cade '54 (lay leader), Harold Blackmon '56, Hyman Jarrett '56, Vernon DeBose '57, James Harshaw '58, Alvin Fant '59, Joyce Wallace '59, Chauncey Black '60, Robert Monroe '60, Henry Briscoe '61, Cedric Hooks '61, Richard Jenkins '61, Carl Johnson '61, Michael Sue Sears '61, Tommy Nash '62, Adrian Young '62, Tommy Sipple '65, Ronald Berry '64, Charles Cofield '64, Leon Manning '64, Victor Williams '64, Sheffer Wynn '64, James Bailey '65, John Gray '65, David Hill '65, Paul Hill '65, Ernest Lewis '65, Donald Moore '65, Linda Robinson Crain '65, Ervin Sims '65, James Meador '66, Leroy Sullivan '66, and Janice Blackmon '67.

SCIENCE

To discover, to explore, to invent, to engineer all for the sake of understanding phenomena and enhancing the quality of life are aims of science. Four Spartans representing this quest are John Hodge '32, W. Michael Rogers '58, Earl Johnson '62, and Walter Rice '64.

John E. Hodge '32 (Phi Beta Kappa), the son of Sumner's third principal, became internationally recognized for his research on browning of food. His work, which added significantly to the body of knowledge on the chemistry of food, was published in the March 1952 edition of the *Journal of the American Chemical Society*. Hodge reviewed and analyzed the browning reaction in dehydrated foods. The chemical reactions produce antioxidants, which have been linked to aging, diabetes, and much more. The importance of his work is evidenced by the award he was given in 1979, twenty-five years after the study's publication, by the Science Citation Index. The article was honored as a "Citation Classic."

Hodge received his bachelor's degree in mathematics and master's degree in chemistry from Kansas University in 1936 and 1938, respectively. He continued postgraduate studies at Bradley University (Illinois) from 1946 to 1960. For more than forty years, Mr. Hodge worked at the U.S. Department of Agriculture Nohem Regional Research Center. He was a visiting professor of chemistry at the University of Campinas in São Paulo, Brazil, in 1972 and an adjunct professor at Bradley University in 1984. Mr. Hodge served as chairman of the Division of Carbohydrate Chemistry of the American Chemical Society in 1964 and remained an active member of a number of scientific organizations, including the Cereal Chemists.

"Having lived in six different cities across this great country," *W. Michael Rogers '58* reflected, "I know of no other high school that can boast the experience or tradition of Sumner High School." He gave unbridled credit to Mr. William Boone, Sumner's revered science and chemistry teacher, for influencing him to pursue a career in science. Under Mr. Boone's tutelage, Rogers won the American Chemical Society Award in the 1957 citywide science fair. His project was "Determining Semi-micro Gas Permabeability Constants." In 1963 Rogers graduated from Mr. Boone's alma mater, Kansas State College of Pittsburg, with a Bachelor of Science degree in chemistry and mathematics. He worked thirty-seven years as a chemist and administrator at the Kansas City District of the U.S. Food and Drug Administration (FDA). During that period, Mr. Rogers worked on different assignments with the United Nations which took him to Kaduna, Nigeria and Papau New Guinea for extended times. In his last position at the FDA, he was Director of the Kansas City District. When he retired, Mr. Rogers started a consulting business targeted to pharmaceutical industries.

After graduating from Sumner, *Earl Johnson '62* was ready to compete on whatever playing field, laboratory, or world market he found himself. Having played football under the capable coaching of Mr. Gerald Hall, taken courses of study focused on science and mathematics from Mr. Paul Brown and Mr. Clarence Turpin, and competed in chess tournaments with rival schools, Earl developed an affinity for working hard and winning. From these experiences, he acquired stamina and resilience that served him well into college and his professional endeavors. Earl received his bachelor's degree in chemistry and physics, his master's degree in organic chemistry, and his doctorate in polymer chemistry.

Although Dr. Johnson spent the bulk of his career in private industry, he advises blacks to be visionary and establish businesses that manufacture products. Dr. Johnson excelled in working with high temperature plastics. He was among the first wave of black professionals that Bendix Corporation hired in 1966, under court decree. He stayed there for four years before he commenced his three-year stint in applied research at Whirlpool. Dr. Johnson worked for DuPont for twenty-seven years as a product or lab sales manager of Teflon. When he retired, he and his wife, who also has a degree in chemistry, opened their own business.

Having cultivated a love for celestial bodies from an early age, *Dr. Walter L. Rice '64*, became an astronomer and worked at the California Institute of Technology's (Caltech) Jet Propulsion Laboratory on the Infrared Astronomical Satellite Survey. He is credited for developing a comprehensive, detailed catalog of infrared celestial objects, which will be used for many years to come. While working on his doctorate, Dr. Rice had the opportunity to be associated with Kitt Peak National Observatory (KPNO) in Tucson, Arizona. KPNO has one of the largest, most assorted collections of astronomical instruments in the world. He also did research at Tucson's National Optical Astronomy Observatory. Dr. Rice has lectured across the United States, England, and Italy.

Other scientists include: Nathan Thatcher '29 (embalmer), Roger S. Whitworth '39 (chemist), Janet Rogers Morgan '57 (bacteriologist), W. Michael Rogers '58 and Linda Boone '65 (microbiologists), and Jackie Johnson Hams '68 (geologist).

Among the alumni who became engineers are: Clarence Jackson, Jr. '42, Arvesta Muzzle Williams, Jr. '43, Donald Harris '56, Ronald Harris '56, Delores Morgan Harris '50, William Jerome Strickland '53, Theodore Marsh '62; Reginald Marsh '63, Franklin Preston '65, Lorenzo Morris '69, LaTanya Starnes Jefferys '73, David Roland '77

Included among the computer technologists and computer and system analysts are: William Jackson '46, Shirley Ross Davis '54, Milton Hill '64, Beverly Reed Mister '64, and Andre Duane Hampton '68.

BUSINESS

Being able to leverage one's talents, skills, and/or interests into moneymaking endeavors is the cornerstone of entrepreneurial success. There are a significant number of Spartans who have excelled as entrepreneurs. Beckwith Horton '56, Willie Davis '60, Henry Taylor '67, and Ronald Harland '68 are among them. Ronald Franklin '64 exemplifies the executive who interfaces the organization and the client for optimal gains.

Beckwith Horton '56 distinguished himself as a promising scientist when he brought home first-place honors from the Greater Kansas City Science Fair in 1955. So, there was no surprise when he earned his bachelor's of science degree in engineering from Kansas University in 1960. What may have been a revelation, though, was when Mr. Horton earned the title of National Small Business Exporter of the Year by the U.S. Small Business Administration in 1991. Indeed, he capitalized on his knowledge, skill, and passion when he founded Juno Enterprises, Inc., and produced and sold electronic computer components around the globe. His business grew from a one-man shop to a firm that hired about two hundred workers and earned millions of dollars in annual revenues. He maintained this company from 1977 until 1997, manufacturing products for such major companies as IBM, Xerox Corporation, and Hewlett Packard. Mr. Horton was acknowledged for his extensive business with France, Germany, Sweden, Switzerland, Brazil, Korea, and Singapore.

Another company that the scientist/businessman/cosmopolite founded was Microtron, Inc., which operated from 1989 to 1999, with over one hundred fifty employees. With a primary focus on manufacturing and selling auto parts, including the "chime" that signals various functions in the car, his company exported products to South American, Canada, and England.

Another competitive entrepreneur was *Willie H. Davis '60.* In 1976 he co-founded Birch & Davis Associates, Inc., a management consultant firm committed to helping the management and staff of numerous organizations improve the efficiency and effectiveness of their operations. His firm grew from a two-person operation into a $75 million organization that employed more than 600 people and that provided services in all 50 states and in 40 countries. For twenty-three years, until its acquisition by a large public corporation, Mr. Davis was dedicated to assisting health care organizations and government agencies that served people overlooked by the traditional health care system. His firm aided organizations in addressing the needs of the poor, the chronically ill, the uninsured, and the addicted.

Mr. Davis completed the Master's of Business Administration program at the University of Massachusetts. Throughout his career, he has worked in many diverse settings ranging from large multinational corporations to small "storefront" operations in urban communities. He has also directed international projects that have taken him throughout the Caribbean and Africa. In South Africa, he directed a four-year effort to provide entrepreneurial training to black South African businessmen striving to survive in an economy dominated by apartheid. Mr. Davis has served on a number of domestic and international boards including Men Against Breast Cancer, the International Hospital for Children, the Victims Rights Foundation, the Washington Tennis and Education Foundation, the Coppin State School of Nursing, Trinity University School of Medicine, and the National Capital Area Minority Business Opportunity Center. He has been honored in Washington, D. C. and in Palm Springs California as "Entrepreneur of the Year."

On the advice of Mr. Lurried Vinson, printing/drafting teacher at Sumner, *Henry Taylor '67* decided to interview with General Motors for a job after he completed college. He was successful. With a bachelor's degree in economics from Kansas University, he entered the corporate world of Oldsmobile. After working there for six years, however, Mr. Taylor decided that he wanted to be on his own. He sold cars and became a manager. Then, in 1981, he seized the opportunity to buy his own dealership just outside of Washington. That was the first of four dealerships he would purchase. Mr. Taylor's was the first African-American new car dealership in the northwestern part of the United States. Although there is no doubt that what he learned in college played a significant role in Mr. Taylor's achievements, he is quick to recognize Sumner as a critical force. "Sumner prepared all of us to succeed in life. The education was tops." Although Mr. Taylor has sold some of his dealerships, he has been committed to making sure that they remain minority owned.

With over twenty-five years of experience at the Xerox Corporation, *Ronald Harland Sr. '69* was more than ready to branch out on his own. After retiring from the corporate world, he was joined by his wife and two sons in founding Evolv Solutions, LLC, in 2002. Evolv Solutions, LLC, is an information technology and document management company. It infuses technologies in its management solutions and recognizes facilities management as its specialty. The company has local, national, and international clients and is expanding its services. By 2006, the fledgling company had been named number one in Ingram's Corporate Report (which ranks corporations in the Greater Kansas City Area) for its over 3,650 percent growth. By spring of 2010, the company boasted winning a prized three-year contract with the U.S. Army Corps of Engineers to scan large quantities of documents digitally. The contract came on the heels of work the company landed with the Kansas City Power & Light Company to manage copiers under its expanding purview. Well on the way to making more and more millions, Harland sees the sky as his only limit.

Under the name MBEConnection.com, Harland has started a social networking business intended to improve small business contracting efforts.

Ronald E. Franklin '64, recipient of Target News' 2006 MAAX Award (Marketing to African-Americans with Excellence) for the "Research Service Executive of the Year," has spent over three decades in the corporate arena. Starting his career as a research analyst for Quaker Oats and ascending to President and Executive Producer of NSights Worldwide, LLC, Mr. Franklin has gained and leveraged a keen understanding of the market place, domestically and internationally. As vice president and director of research at Burrell Advertising in Chicago, he was recognized for establishing a full-service research department and developing a comprehensive information center. At GlobalHue, the nation's largest multicultural marketing and advertising agency designed to meet the unique needs of African-American, Hispanic, and Asian Pacific consumers,

Mr. Franklin has been credited for directing strategic research and establishing prophetic account planning. He is also acknowledged for his work with the United States Trade Department in assisting Ghanaians to expand the country's export capabilities. In 2009, Mr. Franklin was appointed to the Board of Directors of the Advertising Research Foundation (ARF), a non-profit, association that creates, aggregates and disseminates information in the fields of advertising and media. The foundation boasts over 400 advertisers, research firms, media companies, and international organizations.

Mr. Franklin earned his bachelor's degree in mathematics and a master's degree in management from the University of California at Los Angeles.

Other entrepreneurs include: Harold Thatcher '25, James Brown '28, Laura Jarrett Williams '37, William Henry Reaves '38, Emma Jones McIntosh '40, Lawrence Heard '42, James Strickland '47, Marguerite Herron Easley '48, Laverne Walker Washington '48, Edward Watson '49, Joseph Strickland '50, Richard Hopkins '52, Shirley Crowder Lindsay '53, Maurice Herron '53, Stephen Carter '54, Willie Jewell Jarrett '54, Jesse Jones '54, Owen Wilson '55, Keith Maynard '56, Ira Mitchell '56, Sylvester Townsend '57, Jerry Brown '60, Willie Davis '60, Irene Kennard Smith '60, Waymon Guinn '61, Monte Owens '61, Alice Yates Banks '61, Marion Whitehead Brashears '63, Johnny Battles '64, Mary Brown Payton '65, Sherrill Lynn Randolph '67, Joseph Taylor '70, Jonathan Taylor '71, and Larry Harris 77.

Government administrators, business and organization executives include: Willard Shelton '25, Edward Tillman '40, Mildred Bond Roxborough '43, Sarah Daugherty Carr '47, Gloria Smith Despenza '47, Chester Owens Jr. '49, Janet L. Jones '52, Brent Spicer '52, Joanne Collins '53, Lillie Yates Owens '53, Janette Gaines Hopkins '54, Waymon Atkins '56, Jesse Jones Jr. '56, Don Sykes '56, George Ragsdale '58, Charles Weems '56, Frank Henderson '58, Marie Harris '60, Lea Hopkins '62, Earl Johnson '62, Betty Meador Brady '62, Bettye Maddox '62, William Starks '62, Verna Weatherall Mason '62, James Whitcomb '62, David Jones '64, David Manning '64, Robinson '64, Calvin A. Flemmings '65, Wendell Maddox '65, Franklin Preston '65, Gregory King '66, LaDora Pilcher Lattimore '66, Cozetta Payne '66, Thelma J. Whitehead '66, Robert Anderson '67, Marilyn Christian '67, Tamara Collins '68 (Phi Beta Kappa), Maurice Townsend '69,

Gail D. Wilson '69, Jerome Franks '70, Jeffrey Maxwell '76, Willie Kendrick '76, Clarence Boswell '77, and Stephanie Harris '77.

Among the Spartan accountants are: Robert Louis Stevens '23, Detroy Giles '41, James N. Harris '49, Henry Cogshell '61, Theodore Long '62, William (Billy) Owens '62, and Zachary Barber '68.

QUARTER NOTES ON A FEW STANDOUT MUSICIANS

Reaping benefits from Sumner's comprehensive music program and no doubt following their individual interests and talents, a number of graduates became nationally recognized for their musical explorations and contributions. Indeed, Sumner can boast of producing numerous teachers, professors, conductors, instrumentalists, and entertainers, whose works and those of their children and protégés resonate musically throughout the world. Miniscule notes are recorded here to set a framework for their pursuits.

From the Class of 1930, *Nicholas L. Gerren* emerged as the consummate university professor. After receiving his bachelor of music degree and doctorate from Kansas University, he pursued studies at the Moscow Conservatory of Music in violin and orchestra conducting from 1935 to 1937. These accomplishments alone were high notes during a time when economic depression and segregation limited opportunities for blacks. Dr. Gerren spent most of his career teaching budding musicians at the university level. He served as the dean of the music department at Central State University in Wilberforce, Ohio. Highly regarded, he eventually became a consultant in the area of music and fine arts.

Following a career similar to that of Dr. Gerren's in higher education was *William P. Foster '41*. Dubbed the "Dean of America's Band Directors," Dr. Foster has been recognized as one of the most important band directors in the world; he chronicled his philosophy, original marching techniques, and band pageantry in numerous journals and professional newsletters. However, his capstone was *Band Pageantry*, a textbook that has been deemed the "Bible" for marching bands. Dr. Foster is best known for his creative and indefatigable work at Florida A&M University in Tallahassee (FAMU). Under his leadership, the band presented numerous concerts, appeared in three films, commercials, countless newspaper and magazine articles, *60 Minutes*, *20/20*, and the twenty-fifth anniversary national telecasts from Walt Disney World, and *PM Magazine* telecasts. Included in the many recognitions the band received under Dr. Foster is the Sudler Intercollegiate Marching Band Trophy, which is awarded to college marching bands that have made outstanding contributions to the American way of life and have also demonstrated excellence and innovation in music over a period of years. In addition to bringing honor and notoriety to FAMU, Dr. Foster has conducted at Carnegie Hall in New York, Orchestra Hall in Chicago, Constitution Hall in the District of Columbia, Jordan Hall in the New England Conservatory of Music, Interlochen Bowl, National Music Camp, Music Hall in Kansas City, Brooklyn Academy of Music (MENC World's Largest Concert in New York), the Mid-West International Band and Orchestra Clinic in Chicago, and the Kennedy Center in New York.

Prior to his international acclaim as a jazz artist, *Carmell Jones '54* was a valued member of the Sumner High School instrumental music department. He participated in the marching band and other musical groups that provided music for school assemblies, annual concerts, parades, athletic events, and dances. Little did his schoolmates know that they were being entertained by a future professional trumpeter, who would perform with the likes of Sarah Vaughn, Count Basie, Ella Fitzgerald, Billie Holiday, Ray Charles, and Frank Sinatra. No doubt, however, his special sound heard in Horace Silver's still popular "Songs for My Father" brings pleasure and warm memories to those who listened to its birth and development in the music rooms of Sumner. Shortly after graduation, Jones began a four-year stint in the air force, where he played for the 501st Air Force Band. While stationed in Hawaii, he found time to lead his first band and play with blues singer Billie Holiday.

Jones's career kicked off after the service, when he relocated to California. In 1961, he recorded his first release, *The Remarkable Carmell Jones*, for Pacific Records. Ten months later, he produced his second album, *Business Meetin'*. By 1964, Jones had moved across the country to New York City and become a respected member of the Horace Silver Quintet. With this group, he recorded "The Kicker," "Que Pasa," "The Natives Are Restless Tonight," and "Songs for My Father." For his musical contributions to these pieces, he was recognized by *Down Beat* magazine as the "New Star Trumpeter." Jones stayed with the Silver Quintet for less than two years before he ventured to Europe, where he remained for twenty-five years. Before he left, he cut what some consider his most impressive album of all, *Jay Hawk Talk*. While in Europe, he joined the Sender Freies Berlin Big Band and Orchestra as a soloist, composer, arranger, and musical consultant. In 1969, under the Prestige

Records label, Jones released *Carmell Jones in Europe: 1965–66.* For more than two decades, Jones performed throughout Europe. He returned to the United States and resettled in Kansas City, Kansas, in 1980. He released his final album, *Carmell Jones Returns,* in 1983 under Revelation Records. For the remainder of the decade, Jones performed locally and taught at the Charlie Parker Center, the University of Missouri, and Penn Valley Community College.

Another musical genius nurtured at Sumner was *Dr. Reginald T. Buckner '56.* He was an active member in the community, anchored in the church. Most Spartans had no doubt that Reginald would make giant imprints in the world of music, because he was one of the most consistent reasons for the success of major social functions throughout the Kansas City Metropolitan area. He had his own jazz band; they played for dances, concerts, conventions, weddings, funerals, and other special events in Kansas City, Kansas and Kansas City, Missouri.. Getting initial experiences from St. Peters A.M.E., he branched out to Strangers Rest Baptist Church (where he met his wife Sharon Thierry '59) and played for all of its choirs. Dr. Buckner's music was calming, spirited, and always what the listeners wanted and needed to hear. He received the key to the city for the hundreds of hours and tons of talent he shared with the community. After moving to Minneapolis, Minnesota, he stayed connected to the church and became the minister of music at Zion Baptist Church, where one of his fellow Spartans, Reverend Curtis Herron '49, served as pastor.

Dr. Buckner received his formal education at Kansas University: bachelor of music education degree in 1961, master of music education degree in 1966, and doctor of philosophy in music (with emphasis in music education) in 1974. He did postdoctoral work in classical piano at Macalester in Minnesota. Dr. Buckner's evolution into consummate composer of religious, jazz, and secular music was natural and complete. He also published articles on music education, including, "A History of Music Education in the Black Community of Kansas City, Kansas 1905–1954," which was featured in the *Journal of Research in Music Education* in 1982. In this writing, he chronicles Sumner's music teachers, from T. H. Reynolds through Robert N. Clark, and recognizes outstanding music students who came through Sumner. Dr. Buckner edited several books, wrote and arranged many compositions, and continued to perform with groups and individual artists, including the Minnesota Orchestra; Cleveland Civic Orchestra; Benny Bailey, trumpeter in Salzburg, Austria; Nathan Jones '55 and Carmell Jones '54 (Spartans), jazz artists; and songwriter Ralph Blaine. From 1969 to 1989, Dr. Buckner was associate professor of music and Afro American/African studies at the University of Minnesota.

Not surprisingly, the nephew of Dr. William P. Foster, *Mr. Dwight Foster '60,* traces his musical anchoring in general to Sumner and in particular to Mr. Robert N. Clark, Sumner's band director. As a student who wasn't too excited about history, mathematics, or other academic subjects, according to his own testimony, Foster was placed in a curricular program that focused on woodwork and machine shop. One morning, however, Mr. Clark physically removed him from class and from his curricular program. Mr. Clark registered him for the first three periods of the day in music—symphonic orchestra, vocal, and band. Foster shared fond experiences of the Sumner Dance Band with Ralph Ryan, Richard Ryan, and James Weaver on drums; Leonard Smith on bass; Frances Bradley on piano; and Howard Johnson and James Robinson on alto saxophone. "We practiced five mornings a week; we played for assemblies and special programs. If anyone wanted to find me all they had to do was to come into the band room."

Mr. David Jones, music teacher at Northeast, taught Dwight to play the bass clarinet during his early adolescence. But Mr. Clark challenged him to play a variety of instruments and changed his primary instrument to the saxophone, which he has played professionally for more than fifty years. In fact, Mr. Dwight Foster, professionally known as the "Triple Threat," is known for his improvisational talent on the guitar, saxophone, drums, clarinet, organ, piano, vibraphones, and harmonica. He has performed in cities across the United States, including Atlanta, Columbus, Denver, Knoxville, Las Vegas, Los Angeles, Minneapolis, Muncie, Nashville, New Orleans, Orlando, San Diego, Tampa, and extensively in Kansas City. He has played with internationally recognized musicians such as Bobby Bland, Lou Donaldson, B. B. King, Eddy McFadden, Barbara McNair, Frank Sinatra, Grover Washington Jr., and Slappy White. Mr. Foster's musical fortes include jazz, blues, swing, and Latin. He is a member of one of Kansas City's jazz legends, The Scamps. Playing since 1932, this group is one of the oldest jazz groups in the area. As an entertainer, Mr. Foster has touched the hearts of thousands of people; as a teacher, he has helped to guide the lives of countless students. The lessons from Sumner live on.

A few others who continued to thrive musically long beyond the days of Sumner were Algetha Allsbrook '10, Sipora Miller '16, Leah Crump '18, Joseph Ricks '33, Chester White '33, Louis Whitworth '36, Ben Kynard '38 (co-wrote "Red Top"), Amanda Kemp '45, Sylvester Heath '47, John Burris '54, Nathan Jones '55, Elaine Brown Owens '56, William Freeman '60, David Henderson '60, Frances Bradley '62, Marion Love '62, Rosie Thierry Sims '62, Marvin Hollinshed '64, Dianna Howard Kolen '64, Kenneth Heath '65, Paul Hill '65, Errol Robinson '65, Irelene Swain (Salima of New York City) '65, Lester Warner '65, Murline Wright Akers '65, Bernard Johnson '66, and Marquita Meeks Cross '66.

ARTISTS, AUTHORS, AND ENTERTAINERS

Sumner has produced artists, authors, and entertainers. Among the graphic artists are Garland Smith '50 and Dell Godbold '59. Dorothy Kemp Clark '48, Maxine Smith Clair '57 and Gladys Gossett Hankins '60 are counted among the writers. Joanna Featherstone '56 and Steven McKinley Henderson '67 have taken the stage on and off Broadway, as well as writer, artist and comedian Reynaldo Rey '59. Early choreographers who were also entrepreneurs were Dorothy Jean Neal '47 and Irene McLaurin Williams '48.

FIRE FIGHTERS, POLICE OFFICERS, AND MILITARY PERSONNEL

Spartans whose careers placed them at physical risk in the course of protecting the lives of others include firefighters, police and correctional officers, and military personnel. Among the firefighters were: William Freelain '27 , Jesse Hope '42, Kenneth Poole '50 (deputy chief), and Harry Todd '65 (captain). Police and correctional officers included: Victor Talbot '48, Prentice Blackmon '60, Maurice Harris '60, Jewell Thompson '62, Adee Block '64, Louis Johnson '64, Ray McKinney '64, David Abernathy '65, Edward Dryden '65, and Terrence Hall '77. Some military personnel were: Robert Reaves '25, Wilburn Dorris '31, Ernst Foggs '32, Brooks N. Everett '35 (Buffalo Soldier), Walter Brown Sr. '38, Wilson Clemmons '39 (Buffalo Soldier), Geoffrey Martin '44, Vernon Coffey Jr. '46 (military aide to President Richard Nixon – member of the exploratory team to China for the President's historic trip), Jack Curtis '51, Maurice Herron '53, Harold White '54, Shereal McNeal '63, and Howard Berry '64. Though all did not pursue the military as a career, the following alumni were among the highly respected 332nd Fighter Group of the U. S. Army Air Corps, more commonly known as the Tuskegee Airmen: John Young '34, Wilson Clemmons '39 and Donald Jackson '44.

CHAPTER SEVEN

AFRICAN-AMERICAN HIGH SCHOOLS: OTHER PORTALS TO SUCCESS

Teachers and staff must believe that students can learn and demand that they do learn. An unintended effect of the Brown v. Board of Education decision was the taking away of an essential component to the learning process—dedicated teachers and staff.

— Beckwith Horton, Class of 1956

THE PURSUIT OF AN EQUAL EDUCATION

Within the last quarter of the nineteenth century and the first half of the twentieth century, the country saw continuous growth in the establishment of public schools for blacks. Just as Sumner High School of Kansas City, Kansas was unique, revered, and influential in its community, there were other segregated African-American high schools founded in densely populated cities that also set high standards, facilitated change, and provided quality education for their youth. In these communities, it was the firm belief that education was the hope and chief vehicle for attaining equal social, economic, and professional opportunities. These pockets of black society labored hard and long to make sure their children made optimal use of its schools, fully understanding the importance of these institutional emancipators. "Most blacks have been educated in public schools in the United States. In the 30s, 40s and up to about 1954 there were urban black high schools which established and maintained records of excellence."[23] In light of the perils of urban education today, at the beginning of the twenty-first century, the major

---

23   F. Jones , *A Traditional Model of Educational Excellence: The Story of Dunbar High School in Little Rock, Arkansas* (Washington, D.C.: Howard University Press, 1981).

question that comes to mind is what happened. What makes these schools different today than what they were prior to *Brown v. Board of Education*? What happened to the expectations of excellence?

Researchers have tried to determine key elements for the success of black schools of the past. For most African-American communities, the key components were love, structure, discipline, high expectations, and a nurturing environment. Like Sumner, other black high schools began with these elements and were considered successful institutions until the "fallout" of desegregation.

In this chapter, the legacies of nine other schools similar to Sumner are briefly discussed. The immeasurable contributions they made to their communities in the past are cursorily recognized and compared, and a glimpse into their current status is given. Although nominal research has been done on the effectiveness of early African-American high schools, the testimonies to their phenomenal impact are born out in the accomplishments of their graduates. A better understanding of the tangible and intangible factors that made life rich for the students, even when material resources were limited or nonexistent, is gained. A brief history as well as a discussion of commonalities in what made these schools successful will be explored.

Three popular names of early African-American high schools were Sumner, Douglass, and Dunbar. In this review, two schools are named after Charles Sumner, three schools are named in honor of Paul Laurence Dunbar, and one school is named after Frederick Douglass. The three others are named after Arthur H. Parker, Crispus Attucks, and Jean Baptiste Point du Sable, respectively.

Frederick Douglass was a famous African-American abolitionist, women's suffragist, editor, orator, author, statesman, and reformer. Like Douglass, Charles Sumner was a well-known abolitionist and senator who fought for civil rights. Paul Laurence Dunbar, a child of former slaves, achieved international acclaim as a poet, short story writer, novelist, dramatist, and lyricist. He died at the early age of thirty-three but made great strides in his short life. Jean Baptiste Pointe du Sable was the first man of African descent to settle in Chicago and was proclaimed founder of Chicago by the state of Illinois. Crispus Attucks, assumed to be a former slave, was a martyr of the American Revolutionary War. Dr. Arthur Harold Parker served as the principal of the first black high school in Birmingham for fifty years. The founders of each of the high schools reviewed were looking for outstanding individuals with characteristics that would inspire students to greatness as they passed through the halls of their institutions.

Criteria for the selection of schools to review were: (1) the school was located in densely populated African-American communities; (2) the school was generally accepted by African Americans as a school of excellence and was accredited, and (3) the school was established before *Brown v. Board of Education (1954)*.

Figure 7.1   Segregated High Schools: Other Portals to Success

School and Location	Year Established	% Black population of city when established	Date of Original Accreditation	Current Status
Dunbar Washington, D.C.	1870	25%	1929—Middle States Association	Urban segregated high school
Sumner St. Louis, Missouri	1875	52.2%	1911 North Central Association	Urban segregated high school Segregated
Frederick Douglass Baltimore, Maryland	1883	25.3%	1925 Middle States Association 2005 – Accreditation Dropped	Urban segregated high school
A.H. Parker Birmingham, Alabama	1900	49%	1953 Southern States Association	Urban segregated high school
Sumner Kansas City, Kansas	1904	10%	1914 - North Central Association	1978 Closed as high school 1978 Re-opened as magnet high school
Huntington Newport News, Virginia	1912	95%	1931 –Southern States Association	1971 Closed as high school 1971 Re-opened as junior high school 2006 Converted to middle school
Crispus Attucks Indianapolis, Indiana	1927	Less than 10%	2002 - North Central Association	1986 Closed as high school 1986 Re-opened as middle school 2006 Converted to magnet school for grades 6 - 12
Dunbar Little Rock, Arkansas	1929	25.4%	1932 North Central Association	1955 Converted to junior high School 1988 Added magnet school to the junior high program 1999 Converted to magnet middle school
Dunbar Baltimore, Maryland	1940	25%	1940 by Middle States Association	Urban segregated high school
duSable High School Chicago, Illinois	1934	10.2%	1951 North Central accreditation is the same as Wendell Phillips—April 1, 1905	Urban segregated high school

143

CHARACTERISTICS OF HIGHLY EFFECTIVE AFRICAN-AMERICAN SCHOOLS

Jones (1981) reasserts in her well-documented study of Dunbar High School of Little Rock, Arkansas, that most blacks in the United States have been educated in public schools. She identified and drew conclusions on several common characteristics of highly effective African-American schools. Many of these same characteristics were prevalent in the high schools reviewed for this document. They included: (1) strong administrative leadership; (2) a climate of high expectations, where no children are permitted to fall below minimum levels of achievement; (3) an orderly but not rigid atmosphere conducive to learning; (4) a philosophy that makes it clear that pupil acquisition of basic academic skills is the first order of business, taking precedence over all other school activities; (5) flexibility to allow school energy and resources to be diverted in furtherance of fundamental objectives, and (6) frequent monitoring and evaluation of pupil progress.[24]

These characteristics have all been general themes found in comments from alumni from all nine of the institutions and from publications about the high schools. In addition, pride and parent–teacher collaboration were strong elements in strengthening the bonds of the schools and communities; the parental and community support served as a common stabilizing factor. Lucas (1999), in the Huntington school story, observed that parents felt they had a double stake in the school because their children needed a good education from the school and that much of their own social activities were centered at the high school. Pride was taken in the quality of education and the overall value of the institution in advancing social opportunities for everyone in the community.[25]

Sumner High School was established in Kansas City, Kansas, in direct response to the threat of racial violence in the city and a growing demand for the exclusion of African-American students from the local high school. Black parents did not originally agree on a separate high school. Eventually, however, it was their stalwart determination to build and sustain a black high school that rivaled the white high school; one that would provide the highest caliber of curricular and social experiences and become a "bastion of excellence." There are other stories of schools where the African-American community came together and supported the

---

24 Jones (1981). Wilson identifies characteristics of effective schools.
25 H. T. Lucas, *Huntington High School: Symbol of Community Hope and Unity (1920–1971).* (Newport News, Va.: Newsome House, Museum and Cultural Center, 1999).

founding of a segregated school without the pressure of expulsion from an existing predominately white school. For example, parents of the Sumner High School of St. Louis, Missouri wanted a segregated high school and had the support of Charles Sumner himself. A. H. Parker High School of Birmingham provides another such example. Under the leadership of a visionary businessman who proposed an exclusive high school for blacks, the community came together and turned their ideas into realities. Beginning with one room set aside in an elementary school, their struggles resulted in the largest high school for blacks in the world. They were unwavering in their resolve to have the best education possible for their children; they believed it could be and would be attained in a segregated school.

SELECTED HIGH SCHOOLS IN REVIEW

1. Dunbar High School of Washington, D.C., 1870–

African Americans have long played significant roles in the civic, social, and economic life of Washington, D.C., and the nation. In no small measure, Dunbar High School of Washington, D.C., the oldest African-American high school in the country, has influenced those varied roles. Dunbar has produced such renowned leaders as Mary Church Terrell—first black woman to hold a position on the District of Columbia Board of Education (1895), founder of the National Association of College Women, later known as the National Association of University Women (1910); Nannie Helen Burroughs—renowned educator, orator, religious leader, and businesswoman who founded the National Training School for Women and Girls (1909); Carter G. Woodson—second African American to earn a Ph.D. from Harvard (1912), founder of the Association for the Study of African-American Life (1915), originator of *The Journal of Negro History* (1916), and the initiator of Negro History Week (1926); Charles Hamilton Houston—1915 valedictorian of Amherst College, attorney known as the "man who killed Jim Crow" for his strategic role in *Brown v. Board of Education* (1954); Charles Drew—inventor of the blood bank, establisher of the American Red Cross Blood Bank (1940); Edward Brooke—first African American to be elected to the U.S. Senate (1966); Robert C. Weaver—first African-American cabinet official in the United States as secretary of the Department of Housing (1966); and Eleanor Holmes Norton—Georgetown law professor, District of Columbia Delegate to the House of Representatives.

In 1800, African Americans constituted 25 percent of the total population of Washington, D.C.; the majority of these inhabitants were slaves. However, three decades later, a significant number of these former slaves had bought their own and their kinsmen's freedom or had been freed by their slave owners. The city had one of the largest concentrations of free blacks in the United States. In 1835, the rejection of slavery by blacks was so widespread and on such a steady track for total abolition, Congress banned antislavery literature in the District of Columbia, attempting to stem the movement; the ban was unsuccessful. On April 16, 1862, Congress passed the District of Columbia Emancipation Act, freeing all slaves in the city. The passage reflected long-fought battles of blacks to eradicate human bondage; it foretold the vanguard status blacks in the nation's capital would earn on a number of fronts. The act was passed nine months prior to the Emancipation Proclamation of January 1863, which freed all blacks living in states that were in rebellion with the Union.[26] That nine-month head start was a virtual gestation period for the birth of a new spirit of liberation.

Eight years after emancipation in the District of Columbia, Dunbar High School was founded as the Preparatory High School for Colored Youth, the vanguard of black high schools. It was located in the basement of the Fifteenth Street Presbyterian Church. Later, the school moved to 128 M Street, N.W. and became known as the M Street High School. Finally, in 1916, the moniker was changed in honor of Paul Laurence Dunbar and has remained intact since that time.[27] The original school had very poor facilities but prided itself on academic achievements that resulted from a highly qualified and committed faculty. The school's worth was validated by the large number of graduates who went on to college and made influential, nationally recognized contributions.[28] The school's reputation grew so rapidly and expansively that African Americans from near and far moved their families to the area specifically so their children could take advantage of the educational opportunity. Although Dunbar was part of a segregated school system, it functioned as a powerful magnet for black educators seeking employment.

---

26   M. A. McQuirter, *African Americans in Washington, D.C. 1800–1975.* http://www.culturaltourismdc. org/information3949/information_show.htm, reprinted from M. A. McQuirter, *African American Heritage, Washington. D.C.: Cultural Tourism 2003* (accessed August 27, 2009).

27   S. Fitzpatrick and M. R. Goodwin, *The Guide to Black Washington: Places and Events of Historical Significance.* (Washington, D.C.: Hippocrene Books, 1998).

28   Dunbar Alumni Federation, 2006. http://www.dunbaralumnifederation.org/highlights.html (accessed January 10, 2010).

Teachers and principals were extremely well qualified; many of them held Ph.D.s and other advanced degrees. Dunbar may not have been their first choice of a workplace, but most could not find comparable employment in other institutions.[29] Segregation, which dramatically limited career prospects, resulted in the concentration of highly qualified faculty at schools across the nation prior to the early 1960s. This same pattern of forced "cerebral coalescing" would be repeated in many cities across the country and served as the foundation of stellar black schools. While this worked to the advantage of black communities and their youth, it clearly highlighted the great divide in career options and economic opportunities for highly educated blacks. Though these black teachers were not able to fully actualize their potential talents and preparations, they planted fertile seeds in their students who went on to reach heights they could only imagine. Among the early administrators at Dunbar was Mary Patterson, who is recognized as the first black woman to earn a college degree in America.[30]

Although it was unquestionably an outstanding school, Dunbar did not receive its original accreditation until 1929. (Sumner High School of Kansas City, Kansas, which was founded more than three decades after Dunbar opened its doors, received its original accreditation in 1914.) After the early 1960s, Dunbar's reputation began to decline. It rebounded briefly in 1992, when it was recognized by the U.S. Department of Education as a "Blue Ribbon School" for its academic strides. Much credit was given to its Science and Engineering Academy, a magnet program within the school, established in the mid-1980s. Colleges from across the country sought prospective minority students to fill their rosters in science, mathematics, and engineering from Dunbar Academy's rolls. However, the school's historic productivity continued to wane, and therefore so did its esteem

Charles Sumner Lofton, former principal of Dunbar during the civil rights era, voiced observations regarding the decline of Dunbar in the mid-sixties. In an interview, he stated, "The coming of integration demolished the special feelings and spirit of the school. This was at a time when Dunbar was known as an academically rigorous school." Lofton went on to say that he had more influence on students in the segregated environment.[31]

---

29 Dunbar Alumni Federation (2006).
30 Fitzpatrick and Goodwin (1998). First degree earned by a black woman.
31 Dunbar Alumni Federation (2006).

Records show that following desegregation in the sixties and demolition of its original facility in the seventies, the school's prestige diminished significantly. The campus was no longer central to the African-American community. The school has not met academic expectations of the District for more than three consecutive years and is considered "in need of improvement." Today the school is recognized mostly for the success of its athletic teams.

2. Charles Sumner High School of St. Louis, Missouri, 1875–

Charles Sumner High School of St. Louis, Missouri first opened its doors in 1875. It was the first African-American high school west of the Mississippi River and the only high school for blacks in St. Louis until 1927. Sumner has served the St. Louis, Missouri community under the same name and focusing on the same population for over 134 years.

St. Louis and Kansas City, Missouri serve as gateways to the west. During the late 1880s, as people migrated in that direction, St. Louis amassed a population of 350,518; 52.2 percent were of African descent.[32] With such compelling demographics, the Missouri Radical Constitution of 1865, which required all school boards to support black education, was created. Based on the desire for a school and extensive lobbying efforts by the African-American community, coupled with the legislative mandate, the school was established. Its first building was located in an area of town where black children walking to and from school were daily exposed to men being hanged at the gallows. The harrowing images and debilitating messages that must have emanated from this scene were unacceptable. In response to parents' relentless complaints, the school was moved in the early 1880s to its present location.

Like Sumner of Kansas City, Kansas and Dunbar of Washington, D.C., Sumner of St. Louis, Missouri had a rich legacy of outstanding faculty. Most noted among its ranks was the first African American selected to Phi Beta Kappa and the first African-American Ph.D. in physics, Dr. Edward Bouchet. During his tenure at Sumner, Dr. Bouchet served as a science teacher. His accomplishments set the standard for other aspiring educators. A scholarly society has been established at Howard University and at Harvard University in his honor to encourage the goal of excellence in the sciences.

---

32 "Sumner High School" (St. Louis). http://en.wikipedia.org/wiki/Sumner_High_School (accessed July 22, 2009). St. Louis had a large African American population during the late 1900s.

Sumner of St. Louis is noted for producing such outstanding alumni as Arthur Ashe—the first African American selected to play in the Davis Cup, cofounder of the Association of Tennis Professionals, outspoken opponent of apartheid who brought South Africa to the forefront of American society, columnist for the *Washington Post* and *Tennis Magazine*; The Honorable William Clay—first African American from the state of Missouri elected to the U.S. Congress in 1968, cofounder of the Congressional Black Caucus; Dick Gregory—acclaimed comedian, activist, and writer; Robert McFerrin—first black male soloist to perform at the Metropolitan Opera, vocalist for Sidney Poitier in the classic 1959 production of *Porgy and Bess*, recipient of the Lifetime Achievement Award from Opera America in 2003; Robert Guillaume—Emmy Award winner for his role in ABC's *Benson*, star in Broadway hit *Phantom of the Opera*; and many others in the entertainment profession, including Tina Turner, Chuck Berry, Billy Davis Jr., Oliver Lake, and Baikida Carroll.[33]

Like Dunbar of Washington, D.C., Sumner of St. Louis has declined dramatically in prestige. It has not met its academic goals for over three years and has been plagued by a declining enrollment, going from approximately 1,250 in 2005 to less than 600 in 2009. In accordance with the No Child Left Behind Legislation of 2001, state takeover appears imminent.

Frederick Douglass High School and Dunbar High School of Baltimore, Maryland

Two schools in Baltimore, Maryland, further exemplify the ongoing battle of African-American citizens in their quest for high-quality education. Prior to the 1954 Supreme Court decision in *Brown v. Board of Education*, black teenagers in Baltimore were allowed to attend only Frederick Douglass and Dunbar High Schools.

Like Washington, D.C. and St. Louis, Baltimore served as an escape route for runaway slaves and became a haven for heavy migrations of blacks. By 1883, the ex-slaves who had settled in Baltimore were able to obtain a high school education in a segregated facility. However, resources for the school were limited and access to the school was complex. Originally, blacks could only attend Frederick Douglass, the lone black high school. The black population in the city was not centralized, and

---

33 "Sumner High School (St. Louis).

students who lived in other areas of the city had to walk many miles or they could not attend. Although public transportation was available, it was not affordable on a daily basis for most families. It was not until 1940 that a second high school became available for blacks: Dunbar.

3. *Frederick Douglass High School of Baltimore, Maryland, 1883–*

Frederick Douglass High School was organized in 1883 as the Colored High and Training School. Like the Sumners of Kansas City and St. Louis, the high school offered both the high school curriculum and the normal school curriculum, which prepared students to become elementary school teachers. The normal school program separated from the high school and eventually became Coppin State University, an esteemed institution of the Historical Black Colleges and Universities (HBCU).[34] The Colored High and Training School maintained its name until after 1920 when a new building was erected and equipped with a gymnasium, library, and cafeteria. Shortly after moving into the new building (1925), the school's name was changed in honor of Frederick Douglass and no doubt to reflect growing pride in the strides being made at this black institution. Douglass of Baltimore and Dunbar of Washington, D.C. served as the first two black high schools east of the Mississippi River.

Mirroring the success of Dunbar (and Sumner of Kansas City and Sumner of St. Louis), a significant number of graduates went on to college or normal school during the first few decades of its existence. Reflective of the quality of education provided, Douglass High School produced successful alumni who made history on national and international levels. One of its favorite sons was Supreme Court Justice Thurgood Marshall, whose life story is a history book within itself. After receiving world recognition for his brilliance and oratory in *Brown v. Board of Education (1954)*, Marshall was appointed by President John Kennedy to the U.S. Court of Appeals in 1961, and in 1967 he was appointed the first African American to the U.S. Supreme Court by President Lyndon Johnson.

A few other illustrious graduates of Douglass include: Clarence M. Mitchell, renowned lobbyist for NAACP who fought tirelessly for the Civil Rights Acts of 1957, 1960, and 1964, the Voting Rights Act of 1965, and the Fair Housing Act of 1968; he was awarded the Presidential Medal of Freedom by President Jimmy

---

34   "Douglass Senior High School" (Baltimore, Md.). http://en.wikipediaorg/wiki/Frederck_Douglass_Senior_High_SchoolBaltimore,Maryland (accessed August 31, 2009).

Carter in 1980 for his efforts. Several buildings in the state of Maryland have been named in his honor including one in the School of Engineering at Morgan State University, the admissions building at the University of Maryland, and the main courthouse in Baltimore. Juanita Jackson Mitchell, the first black woman to practice law in the state of Maryland, was also a graduate of Douglass, as were Parren J. Mitchell, the first elected black to represent the state of Maryland in the U.S. Congress, the first black to attend graduate school at the University of Maryland; Cab Calloway, famous band leader and singer who broke the color barrier with his appearance on the *Walter Winchell Radio Show* and who starred in such major Broadway and off- Broadway productions as *Porgy and Bess, Hello Dolly, The Pajama Game, Bubbling Brown Sugar,* and *Uptown*; and Veronica Tyler, the accomplished opera singer and professor of voice, who has performed across the world in such acclaimed venues as the Bergen Festival in Norway, the Spoleto Festival in Italy, the New York City Opera, the Metropolitan Opera, the San Francisco Opera House, the Finnish National Opera, and the Teatro la Fenice in Venice; she has worked on faculties of the University of Florida, University of Missouri, Morgan State University, the University of Michigan, and the Peabody Conservatory of the Johns Hopkins University.

One alumnus from the class of 1943 opined, "Our aim was always to be better. In the world, we had to be better. Our motto was Pride, Dignity, and Excellence, and we believed this with every fiber of our being." Although Frederick Douglass received its original accreditation from the Middle States Association in 1951, it has struggled over the last few decades to maintain its academic standing. In 2005, its accreditation was dropped.

Many African Americans feel that what may have hurt Douglass High School the most was *Brown v. Board of Education (1954)* itself. Citizens in Baltimore have expressed that while the court case was intended to improve education for all races, in reality, it was the impetus for some of the best and brightest students to leave the school and attend Baltimore Polytechnic Institute, City and Western High Schools. Teachers from Douglass were also moved to other schools. In 2005, it was reported that less than 50 percent of the teachers at Douglass were certified to teach core subjects. The school has failed to meet yearly progress goals as mandated by the No Child Left Behind Legislation of 2001.[35]

---

35 "Frederick Douglass Senior High School." http//:www.greatschools.net (accessed August 31, 2009).

4. *Dunbar High School of Baltimore, Maryland, 1934–*

Dunbar evolved from an elementary school that began in 1918, transformed into a junior high in 1925, and became a full-fledged high school in 1934. From its beginnings, Dunbar distinguished itself as a leading institution in the community by setting academic standards for students and hiring highly qualified administrators and teachers. The first principal was Carrington L. Davis, a Harvard graduate. Other faculty members were graduates from prestigious universities, including Brown University, Amherst, and Rutgers. Yolanda Du Bois, the daughter of W. E. B Du Bois, was also once a member of the school's outstanding faculty. It is believed that the "underemployed" members of Dunbar's faculty challenged the city of Baltimore for a new school building and openly protested its segregated laws and policies.

> Dunbar High School has a rich history of community involvement. Its role in being the second school for African Americans was vital in its early years. It offered a quality education to many who did not have that opportunity until this school was created. The students of Dunbar played a major role in the desegregation of the city of Baltimore.[36]

Although Dunbar received accreditation in its initial years, the school has not maintained academic integrity. Currently, continued accreditation is in jeopardy. Like the Dunbar of the District of Columbia, Dunbar of Baltimore is recognized for its athletic programs. With a record of 29–0, the 1981–1982 basketball team was ranked first in the nation by *USA Today* and helped shape NBA players Muggsy Bogues (Charlotte Hornets), Reggie Lewis (Boston Celtics), David Wingate (San Antonio Spurs, New York Knicks, Washington Bullets), and Reggie Williams (Los Angeles Clippers). Sam Cassell who played for the Phoenix Suns and served as assistant coach of the Washington Wizards is also a Dunbar alumnus.

Other distinguished Dunbar graduates include: Robert M. Bell, first black chief judge in the Maryland Court of Appeals; Hattie N. Harrison, first African-American woman to chair a legislative committee in the Maryland House of Delegates; Kenneth N. Harris, former city councilman of Baltimore; and Tupac Shakur, prolific hip-hop icon.

---

36 M. Brown and K. Griffin, *Essays by Mandela Brown and Kenneth Griffin.* Research project funded by the Annie E. Casey Foundation. http://www.mdcivilrights.org/DunbarDouglass.html (accessed August 27, 2009).

5. A. H. Parker High School of Birmingham, Alabama, 1900–

A. H. Parker High School opened its doors with an enrollment of eighteen students on the second floor of the Cameron High School in 1900. Originally named the Negro High School and later called the Industrial High School, it was established in response to the demand of black citizens for access to an education for their children. Spearheaded by Dr. W. R. Pettiford, owner of the Negro Penny Savings Bank, this group petitioned the Birmingham Board of Education to support a black high school. Although students were required to pay a fee of $1.50 per month to attend, enrollment had grown to forty-five by the end of its first year. The board appointed Arthur Harold Parker to serve as principal and only teacher of the new Negro High School.

With a strong vocational emphasis, the school continued to grow. In 1904 it celebrated its first graduating class, comprised of fifteen students, and added a second teacher to the staff. In 1910, the school changed its name to reflect its curricular focus and added a third teacher. It was not until 1925 that the Industrial High School was relocated into a building of its own. Still under the guidance of Mr. Parker, the school continued to grow and reached an enrollment of 3,761 by 1946. Not only had enrollment grown, but the curriculum had expanded as well. A rigorous program, which included mechanics, printing, and nursing, was in place. The school became known as the largest school for African-American students in the world.

Mr. A. H. Parker was known for his selfless diligence and care for his students and fellow humans. He sought to instill the principles of humor, pride, and discipline to thousands of black boys and girls. He worked tirelessly to teach them to be caring and devoted to one another.[37] Principal Parker retired after fifty years of service to the school and community; the school was renamed in his honor.

In 1953, A. H. Parker High School received its original accreditation and has maintained it to date. After 1954, when the decision of *Brown v. Board of Education* was reached, many of the best and brightest students left for better-equipped schools elsewhere in Birmingham and its suburbs. Before the decision, the children of doctors and ditch diggers learned side by side. But Parker became a victim of the court decree. The middle-class flight led to a new *de facto* segregation based on class. Even in the midst of flight and the resulting difficult economic

---

37 "A. H. Parker High School History." http://parkeralumni.com/history.htm (accessed September 1, 2009).

times, the school is still a symbol of pride and a "cocoon of excellence" for many in the city of Birmingham.[38] Although Parker met its academic targets for 2008, the rate of graduation prevented it from meeting adequate yearly progress based on the No Child Legislation of 2001.

Outstanding Parker High School alumni include: Oscar Adams, first black to serve as Alabama Supreme Court Justice; Buck Buchanan, former defensive lineman for Kansas City Chiefs, member of the Pro Football Hall of Fame ('90); Nell Carter, Tony Award–winning singer and actress; Lola Hendricks, civil rights activist; Erskine Hawkins, Alabama Jazz Hall of Famer; Alma Johnson Powell, author and wife of former secretary of state Colin Powell; and Larry Langford, former mayor of Birmingham.[39]

6. Huntington High School of Newport News, Virginia, 1919–1971

Efforts to educate black children in Newport News, Virginia predate 1865. During the Civil War, Ft. Monroe, which adjoined Warwick County (Newport News area), became the site of captured and escaped slaves. The commander of the Union Army solicited Mary Peak, a free and educated black, to teach the children of Ft. Monroe to read and write. After the war, blacks settled in this area and elementary schools were built. In the early years, the territory was known for its agrarian economy and families needed older children's hands to help produce the crops. However, by 1912, Negro parents and concerned citizens were convinced that students needed education beyond the elementary grades. They petitioned city officials for a high school. Prior to the actual establishment of a high school, some parents were able to send their children outside of Newport News to get a secondary education. However, the costs were equivalent to a college education and only a few African-American parents could afford to do this.[40]

It was not until 1919 that the city designated a single room for high school students in the John Marshall Elementary School; they named this small secondary accommodation Dunbar High School.[41] Students of Newport News and from

---

38   "A. H. Parker High School. http://en.wikipedia.org/wiki/A.H.Parker_High_School (accessed September 1, 2009).

39   "A. H. Parker High School. http://en.wikipedia.org/wiki/A.H.Parker_High_School (accessed September 1, 2009).

40   Lucas (1999).

41   "Huntington High School—Quick Facts," *Virginia African American Heritage Sites & Organizations.* http://www.aaheritageva.org/search/sitesphp?site_id=605 (accessed August 31, 2009).

surrounding counties came to the "school within a school" to get an education. By 1920, the high school had been renamed Huntington High School in honor of Collis Potter Huntington, a railroad tycoon who founded the Newport News Shipyard. He had given a large tract of land to be used as a playground and athletic field. The "high school" was moved into a four-room structure, Joseph Parker School, and remained there for three years. Lutrelle F. Palmer Sr. became the school's first principal. His salary was supplemented by voluntary contributions. He moved the school and community forward by overseeing the construction of a new school building and graduating its first class in 1923. In 1936, Palmer moved the school into its third building, a three-story brick building at Thirty-fourth and Orcutt.[42]

Lutrelle Palmer, a man of vision and courage, created a rock-solid foundation and a great learning environment for the students. Community and parent involvement was a major strength of his administration. However, when he decided to advocate equitable salaries increased salaries for his faculty that were equitable with their white counterparts, his good record was ignored, and he was promptly removed from his position in 1943. Mr. W. D. Scales became the second captain of the Huntington ship. He was noted as a strict disciplinarian, who quickly gained the respect of his faculty and student body.

Huntington High School served the African-American student population until it closed in 1971, after graduating forty-eight classes. The last high school principal was Mr. Ross Hines. Community thinking was that after the passage of *Brown v. Board of Education,* they would be able to get the additional resources they needed to improve their school. Much to their chagrin and amazement, this did not happen. In 1971, Huntington was converted to Huntington Intermediate School for grades eight and nine. In 1981, it became Huntington Middle School for grades six through eight.

Throughout its history, Huntington High School, which was a five-year high school, received numerous awards and recognitions on the local, regional, and national levels. Its teachers, like many of those in the segregated black high schools in other cities, were highly credentialed and totally committed to ensuring that black students left their classes well prepared for whatever the next challenge presented. The school boasted of outstanding athletic, academic, and music

---

42 Lucas (1999).

programs. The Christmas and spring concerts were sellouts; the football team and track team rarely finished lower than second place in their leagues, and in the 1940s, Huntington alumni boast of being ranked one of the top six high schools in the nation for academic excellence.[43]

7. Crispus Attucks High School, Indianapolis, Indiana, 1927–

Crispus Attucks High School, the first high school built for African Americans in Indianapolis, opened its doors in the fall of 1927. It was named for a former slave killed in the Boston Massacre and is regarded as the first martyr of the Revolutionary War. Like Sumner of Kansas City, Attucks' beginnings were filled with great tension and unrest. With the rise of the Ku Klux Klan after World War I, demands of segregationists, including a delegation of Indianapolis Chamber of Commerce leaders, called for a separate school for African Americans. D. C. Stephenson, grand dragon of the KKK in twenty-three states, including Indiana, was openly supported by local white politicians as he led this racist effort. Prior to this time, African-American students attended any of the three high schools within the city of Indianapolis.[44]

There was great opposition to the ideas and actions of the Ku Klux Klan from the black community. Black leaders, such as Robert Brokenburr and Lionel Artis, formed a civic group called Better Indianapolis League. They were in total disagreement with the concept of establishing an all-black high school. Their position was, "No one section of the population can be isolated and segregated without taking from it the advantage of the common culture."[45] Archie Greathouse, one of the leaders, filed a lawsuit to prevent the School Board of Commissioners' actions but to no avail. The board voted unanimously to go forth with a segregated high school in spite of the suit and fervent protestations.

Moving forward, the Board of Commissioners voted to name the school Thomas Jefferson. But there was an unyielding outcry from the black community, who fought against naming a school designed for black students in honor of a former slave owner. This time their voices were heeded. Crispus Attucks was the name selected. Not unlike the sentiments in the beginning days of Sumner of

---

43 "Huntington High School—Quick Facts."
44 "Crispus Attucks High School Library Factfiles." http://www2indystar.com/library/factfiles/history/black_history/attucks.html (accessed November 20, 2009).
45 "Crispus Attucks High School Library Factfiles."

Kansas City, not all of the black students wanted to attend the new black school. Some wanted to go back to the white schools because of a wider selection of course offerings. But they were forced to return to Attucks.

Throughout the first forty years of Attucks' history, there were major concerns about space and equipment. When the doors of the new school opened one thousand three hundred students enrolled; this number exceeded the building's capacity by three hundred. Nonetheless, they entered, and enrollment continued to soar over the decades. It peaked at three thousand during the 1940s.[46]

Much like Sumner of Kansas City, the establishment of Attucks presented students, for the first time in their schooling, with the opportunity to receive instruction from well-qualified faculty who looked like them. While the faculty at the white schools had minimal qualifications, most teachers at Crispus Attucks had at least a master's degree and many had earned a Ph.D. Blacks could attend Indiana's state colleges and universities, but they could not return to teach in these institutions, no matter how qualified they were; so, many settled to teach in the high school. These highly educated and talented teachers created rigorous standards for their students; they kept the school in high academic, artistic, and athletic standing.

In 1949, school segregation was outlawed in Indiana. However, the student body of Attucks remained almost exclusively black until the 1970s, when busing to achieve racial integration was implemented. As urban areas across the country changed, so did Indianapolis. Students and teachers left the community, and Attucks' enrollment ebbed to the point of almost closing. As fail-safe measures to keep Attucks up and running, it was converted into a junior high school in 1981 and then into a middle school in 1993. In 2006, a creative and promising plan materialized for Attucks to become a magnet school for students interested in the field of medicine. Capitalizing on its proximity to and the resources of Indiana University School of Medicine and hospitals in the area, the school developed a comprehensive curriculum for grades six through twelve. This sheltered six-year program is intended to ensure rigorous and focused instruction and to resurrect the acclaim of excellence.[47]

---

46 http://indystar.com.

47 "Crispus Attucks High School." http://en.wikipedia.org/wiki/Crispus_Attucks_High_School (accessed November 20, 2009).

Graduates of Attucks have made significant contributions in all walks of life. Among their countless number are Julia Carson, who was the first woman and the first black to represent the Seventh Congressional District of Indianapolis in the U.S. House of Representatives; David Baker, who composed over two thousand musical pieces, ranging from jazz and sonatas to film scores, and who has been commissioned by more than five hundred individuals and ensembles, including Josef Gingold, Ruggerio Ricci, Janos Starker, the New York Philharmonic, Fisk Jubilee Singers, Ohio Chamber Orchestra, the Audubon String Quartet, and the International Horn Society for his brilliant work; and Janet Langhart Cohen, writer, model, news commentator, television journalist, who was the first black weather girl for South Carolina's WBBM-TV. As the wife of Secretary of Defense William S. Cohen, Langhart Cohen became known as the First Lady of the Pentagon for her initiatives to raise morale and provide support to military families. Her efforts include the Military Family Forum, the Pentagon Pop concert series, the Secretary of Defense Annual Holiday tour, and an original series of interviews on Pentagon TV, *Special Assignment*. Oscar Robertson, the twelve-time NBA All Star and eleven-time member of the All NBA Team, who was inducted into the Basketball Hall of Fame in 1980 and considered as one of the fifty greatest players in NBA history, is also a graduate of Attucks. As a student, Robertson led his team to state basketball championships in 1955 and 1956. Angela Brown, noted soprano who has performed with the Tulsa Philharmonic, Indianapolis Symphony, Brevard Festival Orchestra, Long Island Philharmonic, Chicago Sinfonietta, Capetown Opera, Dayton Opera, Alabama Symphony Orchestra, Deutsche Oper Berlin, and the National Opera for Paris, is a product of the vocal music program of Crispus Attucks High School.

8. *Paul Laurence Dunbar High School, Little Rock Arkansas, 1929–1955*

Black educators in Arkansas have an outstanding record of working to achieve in spite of the major obstacles of racial segregation. Schools in Arkansas were separated under Arkansas state laws, customs, and traditions in compliance with *Plessy v. Ferguson* (1896) until 1954. Jones' (1981) research on Dunbar High School in Little Rock stands out as groundbreaking information on what made segregated high schools effective. She found the characteristics of this effective school were: (1) strong administrative leadership, (2) high expectations, (3) an orderly but not rigid instructional atmosphere, (4) academic instruction as the first order of business, and (5) frequent monitoring and evaluating of pupil progress. Her publication focuses on the positive experiences and achievements of blacks in Little Rock from 1930 – 1955, prior to the integration of schools. Dunbar was the only public black high school in Little Rock from 1929 to May 1955. It was one of the many black schools financed by Julius Rosenwald, founder of Sears, Roebuck and Company.

After its opening, students came from various parts of Arkansas that provided no black secondary schools to attend Dunbar, which included grades seven through twelve and a junior college. The junior college was organized in 1929 as an extension of the high school. Its development emerged from a desire on the part of the Little Rock Board to establish an institution to provide higher education for Little Rock's young men and women, which would ultimately enrich the cultural life of the community.

For a very brief period, Dunbar was originally called the Negro Industrial High School, reflecting the Tuskegee model of vocational education that was advocated by Booker T. Washington. However protests from and intervention of black citizens advocating academic education rather than manual labor caused an almost immediate name-change. Dunbar was accredited by the North Central Association in 1931-1932.

It was reported in the early 1950s that 60 percent of Dunbar's graduates went to college. This was an unusually high percentage from a high school with an unselected student body. However, Little Rock housed three four-year colleges in addition to the two-year Dunbar Junior College, and the state college for blacks, AM&N College, was only forty-five miles away. This meant that college attendance was quite possible for those students who had aspirations for higher education. However, in May 1955, Dunbar Junior College was abruptly closed by its Board of Trustees, and four months later the high school was converted into a junior high school. In 1988 the junior high established a magnet program to attract a more diverse student body. In 1999, this school became a middle school and retained the magnet program, Dunbar Gifted and Talented International Studies Middle School.[48]

The discrepancies that existed between Dunbar and its white counterpart, Little Rock High School, later known as Central High School, were blatant. Ranging from square footage to textbooks, to teachers' and principals' salaries,

---

48 Jones (1989), p. 15.

Dunbar fell far short of the prototype. The controversy over equal pay for teachers and principals was taken to court, and in 1943 blacks won the case, *Susie Morris, and the City Teachers' Association of Little Rock, an unincorporated Association v. the Board of Directors of the Little Rock Special School District, and Russell T. Scobee, Superintendent of Schools* (Arkansas Supreme Court). This established the requirement of "equal pay based on professional qualifications and services rendered." [49] Dunbar's teachers and principals were more highly qualified than most of their counterparts at Central High School.

Nine black students from Horace Mann High School attempted to enter the white Central High School in September 1957. Their tumultuous experiences at Central in 1957-58 are well-known, and widely publicized as the "Little Rock Nine." In May 1958, Ernest Green was the first African American to graduate from a racially integrated high school in Little Rock. On September 12, 1958, the U.S. Supreme Court ordered the Little Rock School District to execute its entire plan for school integration. Later that month, under mandate from the governor, Little Rock high schools closed for the year to avoid integration. On June 18, 1959, a federal court delayed Arkansas' school closing unconstitutional.

The alumni of Dunbar High School remain determined to honor and keep the legacy of their alma mater alive. A very active alumni organization has existed and prospered since the first national reunion of all classes was held in Detroit in July 1973. Formal organization of the National Dunbar Alumni Association (NDAA) occurred in 1977; the organization was chartered in 1978 in Little Rock, Arkansas. National reunions are held biennially in different cities across the country. As a result of NDAA efforts, in the fall of 1980, Dunbar High School was approved for inclusion in the National Register of Historic Places.

Two books have been published about the school. The first was A *Traditional Model of Educational Excellence: Dunbar High School of Little Rock, Arkansas,* written by Faustine Childress Jones, an alumna, in 1981. The criteria Jones established in her book for effective schools has been used here in writing the Sumner Story. The second book was co-authored and produced by three Dunbar alumni in 2003. It is *Paul Laurence Dunbar High School of Little Rock Arkansas: Take from Our Lips a Song, Dunbar to Thee,* by Faustine C. Jones-Wilson, Erma Glasco Davis, and Bobby Works.

---

49 *Paul Lawrence Dunbar High School, Little Rock: Commemorating a Well-Preserved, Top Quality Rosenwald School.* http://info.aia.org/nwsltr_hrc.cfm (accessed January 5, 2010).

A few of Dunbar's outstanding alumni are: Thomas Bailey Shropshire, former vice President of Phillip Morris & treasurer of the Miller Brewer Company; Dr. Lloyd C. Elam, president of Meharry Medical College; Andrew P. Torrence, president of Tennessee State University; Woodrow Crockett, Tuskegee Airman WWII member of the 199th fighter squadron known as the "Red Tails"; Isaac T. Gilliam IV, highest ranking African American operations officer at NASA; Della McGraw Goodwin, first African-American elected president of the Wayne State University Nurse Alumni Association, Samuel P. Massie, one of the nation's most distinguished chemists and first black professor of chemistry at the U.S. Naval Academy; Don "Golden" Walters, three-year holder of General Motors Corporation's title of "Number One Gold Crest Professional Salesmaster of the World;" James Icelius Chatman, founder and president of Technology Applications, Inc. which provides professional and technical services to federal government agencies with $60 million in revenue and 555 employees; William B. Patterson, first African-American recreation director in Oakland; Lester Monts, renowned educator and ethnomusicologist; Charles H. Long, researcher, teacher and eminent scholar in the history of religion and religious studies; and Lottie Shackelford, first black female mayor of Little Rock, Arkansas.

9. DuSable High School, Chicago, 1934–

DuSable High School has had a great and illustrious history as one of the top academic schools in Chicago, Illinois. Its history is deeply rooted in that of Wendell Phillips Academy High School. Established in 1905, Wendell Phillips opened its doors as a predominantly white institution. The school was named after Wendell Phillips, an advocate of African-American and Native American civil rights, who became leader of the American Anti-Slavery Society. In 1907, ninety black students enrolled and began to change dramatically the ethnic composition of the school. The great migration of blacks from the south resulted in Phillips becoming Chicago's first predominantly African-American high school by 1920.[50] In light of the rapid growth in the high school and its surrounding community of Bronzeville, more space was needed. A new school, which was called the New Wendell Phillips, opened during the 1934–1935 school year.

---

50   "DuSable High School." http://en.wikipedia.org/wiki/DuSable_High_School (accessed November 20, 2009).

In 1936, the name of the new school was changed to DuSable in honor of the first person of African descent to settle in Chicago. Jean Baptist Pointe du Sable was a Haitian fur trader who built the first permanent, nonindigenous settlement of Chicago at the mouth of the Chicago River. In 1968, the state of Illinois proclaimed du Sable as the founder of Chicago.

The original school and its "annex" were highly successful and became recognized for stellar academic, athletic, and music programs. Wendell Phillips received its original accreditation in 1905, and because of DuSable's close connection with Phillips, it claimed the same original accreditation date.[51]

During the late twenties and thirties, Phillips established itself as a great basketball powerhouse. In 1929, the school's team, the Savoy Big Five, became the nucleus of what would become the Harlem Globetrotters. The basketball prowess carried over into the DuSable era; NBA players Paxton Lumpkin, Maurice Cheeks, and Mitchell Moseley are among its graduates.

DuSable's incredible teacher, Captain Walter Henry Dyett, brought world recognition to the school's outstanding music program. It was not coincidental that so many young people who studied under Dyett became renowned musicians. He had unquestionable influence in the musical careers of such jazz greats as trumpeters Sonny Cohn and Gene Jug Ammons, bassist Fred Hopkins, percussionist/drummer Warren Smith, saxophonists Johnny Griffin and John Gilmore, vocalist Johnny Hartman, pianist and vocalist Nat King Cole, and Grammy Hall of Famer Dinah Washington. Over his thirty-year tenure, Captain Dyett was recognized for having touched more than twenty thousand students' lives through his concert and marching bands and other music programs. In 2008, the jazz community of Chicago paid homage to his extraordinary works by erecting a statue on the campus of DuSable High School.[52]

In 1994, physics teacher Bennett Brown worked with NASA on an education grant to make DuSable the first high school to be connected to the Internet. This process paved the way for other high schools to be connected as well.

However, the overall excellence that once characterized DuSable had long faded. Poor academic achievement, reduced graduation rates, poor attendance, and

---

51 "DuSable High School."

52 R. Wang, "Posted," *Captain Walter Dyett*. http://www.chicagojazz.com/thescene/captain-walter-dyett-86.html (accessed January 10, 2010).

poor performance on state assessments were all indicators of the decline. Living in an impoverished, high-crime area, students experienced innumerable accounts of violence that textured every aspect of their lives. To combat the psychological impact of their experiences, the Urban Ecology Sanctuary was established. It serves as a model for students to experience healing from the multitude of psychological illnesses that confront them. Addressing the psychological needs helps ready students' minds and emotions for focusing on and meeting academic expectations. The sanctuary is located in a courtyard at DuSable, providing a place where young people can reflect on their loss, regain a sense of purpose, and reconnect to the natural world around them. The sanctuary shows how architecture and landscape architecture can buffer the worst effects of social disruption.[53]

Another outstanding teacher, alumnus, and community activist, Dr. Timuel Black, helped lead the way in stemming the decline of the school. At the age of ninety-two, he recalled what it was like being a student at Wendell Phillips and DuSable High Schools. He spent those years in a "nurturing and stimulating environment." He learned from highly qualified teachers, who respected him and encouraged him to go as far in life as his talents would take him.[54] Dr. Black identified teachers such as George Dorsey, Avery French, Mary Herrick, and Mildred Bryant Jones as a few of the role models who encouraged him to become an educator. As vice president of the DuSable Alumni Coalition, he was instrumental in getting the school to upgrade and restructure its programs to better meet students' needs. DuSable has been reorganized into three different programs: the Bronzeville Scholastic Institute, the Betty Shabazz International Charter School, and the William Preparatory School of Medicine. More individualized and focused attention on students is expected to result from this reorganization.[55]

Other outstanding alumni of DuSable High School are: Harold Washington, first black mayor of Chicago; John E. Johnson, founder and CEO of Johnson Publishing Company, creator of *Ebony* and *Jet* magazines, first black to make Forbes 400 list of wealthiest people; Don Cornelius, creator, producer, and host of *Soul Train*, one of the longest running TV shows; Ella Jenkins, folk musician who has appeared on the TV shows *Sesame Street*, *Mister Rogers*, and *Barney and Friends* and

---

53 P. Alt, "Death and Rebirth in Chicago: The DuSable High School Urban Ecology Sanctuary." *Architectural Research Quarterly* (1999): 3.321–334.
54 C. D. Durham, "Timuel D. Black, Bronzeville's Venerable Historian (Hyde Park Historical Society: Chicago, Ill., 2004).
55 Durham (2004).

is the recipient of the Grammy Award for Lifetime Achievement for her children's album; John Elroy Sanford, aka Redd Foxx, Golden Globe–winner for best TV sitcom; and Alonzo S. Parham, the first black to attend West Point.

SOME CONCLUSIONS ON PORTALS TO SUCCESS

The Supreme Court's landmark decision in *Brown v. Board of Education (1954)* brought irreversible change to public schooling. It opened the path to integration and made possible equal access to educational opportunities for children and youth throughout the nation. That was the goal. However, there were repercussions of the law that are not often expressed but are sorely felt by African Americans who were once relegated to segregated communities. Those visionary families and community leaders, who believed in education as the great equalizer and who labored long to build and maintain stellar schools for their children, have painfully witnessed the demise of their coveted institutions over the last fifty years.

Each high school in this "story" once served as a source of hope and a "bedrock" of its community. Yet today, most of these institutions are failing to meet the needs of their youth. Despite increased funding, improved facilities, and imposed academic standards (mandated by No Child Left Behind Legislation of 2001), Dunbar of the District of Columbia, Sumner of St. Louis, Douglass and Dunbar of Baltimore, and DuSable of Chicago are academic blights. Huntington of Newport News and Dunbar of Little Rock were converted into middle schools. Sumner of Kansas City (grades nine through twelve) and Attucks of Indianapolis (grades six through twelve) were integrated and converted into magnet schools. DuSable has been converted into smaller learning communities. The magnet school and academy concepts show promise. However, A. H. Parker of Birmingham was the only high school that survived as it was originally designed to serve a majority of African-American students effectively. What happened?

Alongside the socioeconomic changes facilitated by Title 7 of the 1964 Civil Rights Act and the 1965 Housing Act, the *Brown* decision was a major impetus for some of the best teachers and most motivated students to seek opportunities or to be involuntarily transferred elsewhere. Title 7 dictated that employment vacancies would be filled without regard to discrimination on the basis of sex, age, national origin, religion, or gender. The Housing Act outlawed discrimination in the sale and purchase of property. These laws abetted the devastation of black communities; schools were no exception. Teachers from the formerly segregated school system left for other schools and to become a part of the integrated corporate arena. The exodus of teachers, students, and other community members created huge economic, physical, and social voids in the community. Many of the all-black schools that were once pillars of excellence under segregation became unwitting victims of black flight and inferior education under integration.

Who could have foreseen the devastating repercussions to come? Who could have imagined the impact of removing economic diversity within the race? Can the tide be turned? Can the schools be revived? Can the differences between the schools of yesterday and the schools of today be reconciled? Can the unexpected consequences of the law be ameliorated? Can the "bastions of excellence" of decades past become guiding stars for generations to come? Not unlike Jones's findings,[56] all of the schools in this review had some major commonalities that contributed to their success: (a) highly qualified teachers and principals, (b) high moral and academic standards, (c) support of parents and the community, (d) multiple opportunities for students to develop their talents and minds, and (e) self-engendered discipline.

The models of the past, found in this chapter, validate many strategies proffered today to build and sustain effective schools. The challenge is to revive, modify, and implement them to serve the students of today. They, too, deserve schools that prepare them to navigate and negotiate the world; they, too, deserve to claim educational legacies of success.

---

56 Jones (1989).

CHAPTER 8
CLOSING THOUGHTS BUT NOT THE FINAL CHAPTER

As we close the first volume of an unfinished story, the Writing Team hopes the spirit and essence of the work has been realized. We knew there was a story to tell – a collective experience that had powerful, far-reaching affects on our lives. Memorializing the time, people, and place that helped give birth and nurture a sense of who we are, and ultimately became, was our mission. Each time we came together, we were sobered by the magnitude of this project. We struggled with how to frame the story. To what depth should various parts be covered? What are the critical topics to be addressed? Are the general comments and perspectives of alumni respondents being accurately conveyed?

Although we wrestled with these questions and other issues, we would not allow our concerns to divert us from the goal. We considered several options, but decided to use the structure and format contained in the finished product presented here. We agreed that the story was not finished, but that there had to be an "end point" of this first iteration. We feel that we have honored an incredible institution and the key players who established and sustained it. We also sought to provide evidence of how the school prepared its graduates to excel in all fields of endeavor—but with thousands of graduates, we weren't able to include everyone.

The next chapter will come from other former Spartans, and their children. For names, events, categories, and whatever else that was left out, we ask that you abridge and continue this first volume in a second edition. We envision a second volume being written about and perhaps by the offspring of Sumner High alumni, the "Second Watch," to show how positive and far-reaching the tentacles of educational excellence have been and can continue to be.

Next Chapter

Again, there is no way for the Writing Team to have included all of the personal accounts that Sumner alumni have shared, nor noted every significant event that has transpired over 73 years. However, we recognize and honor the fact that every alumnus has a story, a personal chapter that deserves to be told. For this reason, we have included this final section of the book, My Recollections of Sumner High School, space reserved for interested alumni to write their individual memories of people and events of personal significance. In so doing, family, friends, and progeny will have the benefit of experiencing, in some small measure, just what it was like to be a part of that historic institution of learning called Sumner High School.

My Recollections of

Sumner High School

Kansas City, Kansas

Name _____ Class of _____

Dedicated to _____

My Recollections of Sumner High School

_____

_____

_____

_____

_____

_____

_____

_____

_____

_____

_____

_____

_____

_____

_____

_____

_____

_____

_____

_____

_____

_____

_____

_____

_____

_____

_____

_____

_____

_____

_____

_____

EPILOGUE

Formal education is dependent on numerous factors; highest among them are strong, visionary administrators, and dedicated, capable teachers. Teachers must believe that students can learn and demand that they do so. With this thought in mind, what can be done with what was learned about the educational experiences at Sumner? How can the standards and expectations established by teachers of the past be replicated for future generations?

Sumner High was formed because of the racial climate of the early 1900s. The successful effort to force black students into a segregated school created an unintended "citadel of excellence." It also brought about a greater sense of community.

Due in part to segregation, Sumner High was staffed with dedicated, well-educated, black teachers. They demanded excellence from their students. The high rate of student success shows how teachers can propel students forward against all odds. Sumner's success also shows that segregation, per se, does not mean inferior education. In spite of the U.S. Supreme Court ruling in *Brown v. the Board of Education*, segregation or the lack of integration of schools was and is not the root cause of poor education.

A devastating effect of *Brown v. the Board of Education* was taking away talented teachers, an essential element to the learning process. The gradual exit of this force ultimately led to the decline of high expectations and academic performance of students. *The Sumner Story* details many aspects of the history of an important institution of Kansas City, Kansas, including the impact of its outstanding faculty. It is a history that must not be eradicated by silence and apathy.

The mandate to inform the future of the past has commenced. Through this chronicle, the critical role of quality education is acknowledged. The challenge of attaining it again is proffered.

— Beckwith Horton ('56)

MEET THE AUTHORS

Wilma F. Bonner, Editor

Wilma F. Bonner is currently the Director of Teacher Education at Howard University. She had an extensive career, spanning thirty-seven years, with the District of Columbia Public Schools (DCPS). She was a teacher, principal and central office administrator. In the position of Assistant Superintendent of Senior High Schools, Dr. Bonner played a key role in facilitating the work of the Blue Ribbon Commission on Senior High Schools (2002) which recommended comprehensive measures to improve academic achievement and the overall climate in all DCPS high schools. In her last position in DCPS, Assistant Superintendent of Curriculum and Instruction, Dr. Bonner supervised the adoption and implementation of new learning standards in reading, mathematics, social studies and science. She also chaired the committee that developed the new promotion and graduation requirements for DCPS in spring 2007. She is married to Michael V. Bonner. They have two adult children and four grandchildren.

Sandra E. Freelain

Sandra Freelain received a Master's Degree in Public Administration from the University of Colorado and served as Housing Analyst for the Department of Housing and Urban Development in Washington, DC for 20 years. "The values I have and my straightforward approach to problem solving are by-products of my Midwestern background which I deeply cherish. As part of the Sumner Writing Team I gained a deep respect and renewed gratitude for the collaborative efforts of the administrators, educators and community that established and sustained Sumner High School for seven decades. My retirement in 2007 has provided an impetus to pursue varied interests, including taking piano lessons, traveling abroad, and "spoiling" two lovable cats."

Dwight D. Henderson
LLC, Attorney

Dwight D. Henderson graduated from Sumner High School in 1963. He served as senior class president. Upon graduation he received a basketball scholarship to Kansas State Teachers' College, Pittsburg, Kansas. He graduated from Pittsburg with a BA degree in English and a minor in science. He received a scholarship to Kansas University School of Law, Lawrence, Kansas and graduated with a Juris Doctor Degree in Law. Dwight passed the bars in the states of Kansas and Texas. He received the Reginald Heber Smith Fellow and practiced law with the Houston Legal Foundation, Houston, TX. He became Director of the Wyandotte County Legal Aid Society, Kansas City, KS. He worked as a project attorney for Standard/Amoco/British Petroleum Oil Company. Dwight continued with the corporation until his retirement--specializing in contract and labor law. He is married to the former Phyllis M. White. They have two adult sons, two daughters-in-law and five grand dogs. He loves golf.

Johnnieque Blackmon Love
LLC, Manager

Johnnieque Blackmon Love's professional career spans forty-three years of public education. Her current position is that of Coordinator of Personnel Programs in the University of Maryland Libraries, College Park, Maryland, she has served in this position since 2001. Her career began as a classroom teacher in Jefferson County Public Schools of Colorado. After seven years she found a new career when asked to serve as school resource specialist. She received her first master's degree in Library Media Education at the University of Colorado in Denver in 1977, and a second master's in Information Management in 1984, from the University of Denver, the same year she moved back to Kansas City. As doors opened to librarianship she has been able to work on all levels with the exception of middle school. As the first Diversity Librarian at the University of Kansas, she provided leadership in developing diversity initiatives and program implementation for the KU Libraries. In 1998, she took a position at Texas A&M University serving as Education Librarian.

In addition to family, one of her greatest joys has been serving as one of the former presidents of the Sumner High School Alumni Association. She has worked to continue the efforts of the founders, the Class of 1930, in preserving the legacy of Sumner High School. She attests, "This publication is not only the Writing Team's dream but stands firmly on the founders' shoulders as they developed the foundation for the work. As the Manager of the Sumner Writing Project Team, LLC, it has been more than just a joy. It has been monumental in reward to find the right team members and to work with our distinguished alumni and underwriter in bringing to reality this publication."

Eugene M. Williams

Eugene M. Williams' professional career spans 40+ years, serving in the capacities of teacher of English and career counselor on the high school and college level. He also served as administrator of two federal programs based out of the University of Kansas: Teacher Corps and Upward Bound. As Co-Director of Values Education for the District of Columbia, he orchestrated a district-wide initiative to infuse a values awareness curriculum throughout public schools in the District of Columbia. Williams then served as educational consultant for the government of Saudi Arabia with the Department of Interior (Riyadh, Saudi Arabia) followed by an educational consultancy with the Department of Education at the Embassy of Saudi Arabia in Washington, D. C. More recently, Mr. Williams has served as career transition counselor for two federal agencies in the District: Geo-Spatial Administration (GSA) and the U. S. Government Accountability Office (GAO). Mr. Williams continually volunteers with community organizations that empower and inspire people toward self-sufficiency and personal development.

Sumner Writing Project Team, LLC
Website: http://www.sumnerwritingproject.com

APPENDIXES

1. History of the *Sumner Courier*

2. The Sumner Song

3. Final Tribute to Sumner High School and Northeast Junior High by Students, May 19, 1978

4. Spartan Mascot

HISTORY OF THE SUMNER COURIER

Sumner High School *Courier* began as a four-page, five-column monthly newspaper. From 1912 to 1921, the school's paper was known as the *Sumneriana* and was sponsored by a faculty group. In a 1921 faculty meeting early in the year, the faculty decided by popular vote that the newspaper's name would be changed to the *Sumner Courier*.

Early on, the paper had been published in different ways. At one time, the copy was sent to a public printer, who did the typesetting, while the makeup was done either by the principal or a teacher; it was printed by the printing department of Wyandotte High School, with Mr. J. A. Hodge doing the makeup in the evenings. In 1935, the paper was put back on the plan of being sent to a public printer. Firms that have been employed by the school are: Gray's Printing Company, the Kansas Plainsdealer, the Kansas City Typsetters Company, the E. R. Printing Company, and the Goodnight Printing Company.

The size of the *Courier* has varied from two wide columns on a page, the size of the Sunday school leaf, to a six-page paper of five columns each. In 1935, the size of the paper went to four pages, with five columns to the page. The method of editing the paper was also diversified. In the first period, the teachers would send their news items to the teacher-sponsor of the paper, who did all of the editing. As time progressed, more student involvement was given; each room had a special reporter, who would send the news to the teacher-sponsor. The third method of editing was when the student body elected an editor for the staff newspaper. The method of editing used for the paper until the closing of the school was done by the Journalism Department.

During the years 1936 to 1978, the name of the newspaper was also changed to reflect the times as well as student journalistic decisions. The *Courier's* names have been: (1) *The Courier*, (2) *The Sumner Courier*, (3) *Voice of Spartantown*, and (4) *Courier: Sumner High School, Kansas City, Kansas*. The last publication, May 24, 1978, was called the last name.

Writers of the history of the school in 1935 stated, "Nothing in school has a greater influence than the school newspaper. It fosters school spirit, teaches its workers to shoulder responsibility and gives an outlet into the business field, gives primary training into the journalism field and teaches the person who has no desire to be a journalist or continue work in any of its branches to appreciate the newspaper and its work. The paper also forms a bridge between the school, the home and the local community." School newspapers and journalism have come a long way. These words are true today with one addition to reflect progress: the advancements of technology and computers and the pivotal role they play as tools for journalism and publishing.

Figure A-1 Sumner Courier

SUMNER COURIER

Volume XXII, No. 8   SUMNER HIGH SCHOOL, KANSAS CITY, KANSAS   MAY, 1957

Honor Society Picks Eleven Members

Top Scholars Recognized in School Ceremony

Eleven students were installed by the Sumner chapter of the National Honor Society in ceremonies in the auditorium April 30.

Thomas Jones, junior, opened the program with a piano solo, "Tarentelle." Following a musical reading by Marlene Meeks, "Sunset Bridge," the chapter choir sang "One Little Candle."

Installed were the following students:

Seniors: Doretha Gaines, Naola Hughes and Marvin Trammel. Juniors: Shirley Bunks, A. Portia Davis, Lelond Holbert, Thomas Jones, Michael Rogers, Gerry Weaver, Lora Whitaker and Christine Williams. Sophomore pledges: Carole Arnold, Milton Bledsoe, Sheila Breckenridge, Rosalyn Browne, Ora Bell Carter, Sarah Cogshell, Florine Cowan, Elvin Donald, Bernice Hogan, Wanda Hogan, Anita Hopkins, Delores Johnson, Marva C. Love, William McCasted, Anita McBride, Barbara McClinton, Marlene Meeks, Samuel Nero, Odell Register, and Karen Sears.

In charge of the installation program were the following seniors: Thomas Mason, Mary Cannon, Freddie Harris, Maxine D. Smith, Janet Rogers, John Hodge, Milicent Bledsoe, Jean Norwood, Elaine Arnold, and Patsy Fulcher.

Miss Geraldine Roberson gave the history of the Honor Society and the Sumner chapter. Pins and cards were distributed by Mr. S. H. Thompson, principal.

Sumner Science Fair Participants Rank High for The Past Six Years in Greater Kansas City Fair
By Barbara Rice

When Patricia Wayne Caruthers won the Science Fair this year, it sent your reporter to the files to run down this old Sumner tradition that began six years ago.

Sumner's first participation in the science fair was in 1952. That year the school had one of three top winers, Arvey Andrews. Arvey made a homemade oscilloscope which transformed light into sound.

Along with the two other top winners, he was sent to Washington by the Kansas City Star to enter the National Science Fair.

Among the school entries in 1953 Sumner had two that took the two top awards. Daniel H. Wilson won the top boy award with his project on "The Complex Field of Nuclear Forces," which visualized in a demonstration many different switches, light bulbs and reflectors.

Shirlee Ross won second place and the top girl prize with her pint-size organ.

Unsuccessful in 1954

In 1954 Sumner was unsuccessful in having a top winner, however Mary Bedford was a good runer-up in the physical sciences division with her poto-electric seismograph.

As 1955 drew toward the end of April, Sumner was very well represented again. For the second year both top boy and girl awards were captured by Sumner students. Myrna L. Thomas was the top girl winner with an exhibit entitled "Son-a-Tron," a mechanism that produced electronic sound. Beckwith Horton, top boy winner, won with his original creation called "Photographic Printing by Photosynthesis." Beckwith worked on this project for two years.

In 1956 Sumner won again. Norma Cole and John L. Hodges represented the school well. Norma made an electrametric tritrimeter which calculated the strength of a solution by measuring its resistance to an electric current. John's winning entry with a device to measure the normal burning temperature and velocity of a Bunsen burner. The two students were sent to the National Science Fair in Oklahoma City.

To bring us to the present, Sumner is still winning. This year the judges were really in hot water. The projects were so cleverly and perfectly constructed that the biggest job in the science fair was for the judges to come through with a top boy and girl winner.

The top girl was Patricia Caruthers, a Sumnerite, as earlier stated. Last year's winner, John Hodge, lost by one vote the position of top boy again.

Top Girl From Sumner

The tradition began with Shirlee Ross in 1953 and has thus continued. No other school has yet produced a top girl winner in the Greater Kansas City Science Fair.

So far Sumner has shown a very high standing in the scientific field, and with that old Sumner spirit, its students give every indication of continuing to win.

Throughout the years the sponsers have been Mr. William Boone, Mr. William Smith, Mr. R. R. Mansfield and Mr. E. A. Taylor.

Graduation Hour Nears for Seniors

May 23 Exercises Will Begin at 8 o'Clock

Between 195 and 200 seniors will receive diplomas at the Sumner high school commencement exercises May 23 at the Memorial Hall located at Seventh and Barnett. The program will begin at 8 o'clock.

Baccalaurente services will be held Sunday afternoon, May 19, at 2:30 in the Sumner auditorium. The Rev. Martin E. Nees, pastor of the Faith Lutheran Church, will deliver the Baccalaurente sermon.

Nine on Symposium

In the commencement program, nine graduating seniors will comprise a symposium for a discussion of the general theme "The Present Is Our Challenge." Areas of discussion and speakers are Patsy Fulcher and Freddie Mae Harris, citizenship; John L. Hodge and Marvin Trammel, research; Maxine D. Smith and Geraldine Love, education; Thomas Mason and Janet Rogers, freedom. Martha Jo Woods will serve as chairman.

Music for both programs will be furnished by the choir and orchestra directed by Mr. Oyarma Tate and Mr. Robert N. Clark respectively.

Superintendent of Schools F. L. Schlagle will speak briefly, while a member of the Board of Education will present diplomas to approximately 200 seniors comprising the largest graduating class in the school's history.

SCIENCE FAIR WINNERS—Pictured above are Sumner's winners in the Sixth Annual Greater Kansas City Fair.

Patricia Caruthers (left) won the top girl award with her entry, "The Brownian Movement." Mr. William Boone was her sponsor.

John L. Hodge (second) won the Westinghouse Electric award for the second straight year. He won this award with his project, "Vapor Phase of Chromatography." He also won first place in the physical science group.

Gerry Weaver (third) won second place in the senior biological science group for her experiment, "Extraction of Penicillin from Air Molds." She also won an award from the Scientific Research Society of America.

Lelond Holbert (right) won second place in the physical science group with his experiment, "Zeeman's Effect." Mr. William Smith was his sponsor.

Figure A-2 Sumner Song Verses

In recognition of the accomplishments of Northeast Junior High School and Sumner High School in the Kansas City, Kansas community, the Optimist International Club held a final tribute on April 16, 1978. The Sumner Concert Choir and Stage Band performed at the Tribute. The following songs were part of that tribute.

TRIBUTE TO NORTHEAST JR. HIGH

Dedicated to Former Students and Faculty

Whenever we think of years gone by,
And good old days well spent;
Our minds' relate back to Northeast,
And all the joy she lent.

We cannot cease remembering,
Her strength in ties that bind;
With her solid-truth foundation,
She surely was one-of-a-kind.

Her windows boarded and nailed;
And in our hearts, and mind, and soul,
We honored her colors Blue and White,
And her Motto: "BE THE BEST";

Her Dragon teams helped fill our dreams,
With blissful happiness.

We did not willingly let her close,
For she held Black pride in us;
We talked-and met —and protested loud,
We put up quite a fuss.

But yet her doors were snuggly shut,
We felt that we had failed
We must not let our roots decay,
From things we hate and fear;

We must remind and ask ourselves:
WHERE DO WE GO FROM HERE???>

Song written by
Marilyn DeGraftenreed Thompson
(Excerpts from the final edition of Sumner Courier, May 19, 1978)

SALUTE TO SUMNER HIGH

Dedicated to all Sumnerites

There comes a time in all our lives,
We're asked to prove our worth;
And trace our steps through sands of time,
From "what is" – back to birth.

Of course there're things we know not of,
And things we have forgot;
And memories of things that "were,"
But now those things are not.

We're called, at hand, to reminisce,
Our Sumner High Schools days
A special time, event, or class,
Our "Sumnerite" stylish ways.

Others recognize what Sumner means,
To us who were a part;
Our heritage, embedded roots,
An insignia in our heart.

And yet, it's coming to a close,
But our pride will still live long;
We're still remember Orange and Black,
And sing our old school song.

For Sumner produced strong character,
And Black culture at its best;
And many greats, with many skills,
Outstanding from the rest.

It's Motto: "Be Prepared" has been,
A theme we took in stride;
"Conquer or Die," our battle cry,
Is what made Sumner High.

"Let Me Call You Sweetheart,"
For we truly love you dear;
For you have proved your worth to us,
For this we shed a tear.
Our happy days were spent with you,
Inside your field and walls;
We still can hear our whispers,
And our footsteps in your halls.

We've cheered the Spartans to victory,
And we've rallied at Grand affairs;
Debate teams, Science or Literature,
Each Sumnerite did its share.

The gift of metamorphosis,
Now, Sumner can proclaim;
For we've always had potential,
In our academic aim.

There's nothing new under the sun,
Nor nothing left worth seeing;
For Sumner High has blossomed out.
She's only come into being.

Song written by
Marilyn DeGraftenreed Thompson
(Excerpts from the final edition of Sumner Courier, May 19, 1978)

Figure A-3   Sumner Song Chorus

Figure A-4   Spartan Mascot

BIBLIOGRAPHY

BOOKS

Fitzpatrick, S., and M. R. Goodwin.(1998). *The Guide to Black Washington: Places and Events of Historic and Cultural Significance*. Washington, D.C.: Hippocrene Books.

Gatewood, W. B., Jr. (2000). *Aristocrats of Color, The Black Elite, 1880-1920*. Fayetteville: University of Arkansas Press.

Greenbaum, S. D. (1982). *The Afro-American Community in Kansas City, Kansas: A History*. Kansas City, Kansas: Brennan Printing Co.

Lucas, H. T. (1999). *Huntington High School: Symbol of Community Hope and Unity (1920–1971)*. Newport News, Va.: Newsome House, Museum and Cultural Center.

Mobiley, A. E. (1985). *The Educational Crisis*. Pompano, Fla: Exposition of Florida.

Wilson, Jones-Childress, F. (1989). *A Traditional Model of Educational Excellence: The Story of Dunbar High School in Little Rock, Arkansas*. Washington, D.C.: Howard University Press.

DISSERTATION

Lawrence, D. (1998). *The Impact of Local, State, and Federal Government Decisions on the Segregation and Subsequent Integration of Sumner High School in Kansas City, Kansas*. Lawrence: University of Kansas School of Education.

ARTICLES

Alt, P. (1999). "Death and Rebirth in Chicago: The DuSable High School Urban Ecology Sanctuary." *Architectural Research Quarterly*, 3. 321-334. doi 10.1017/S1359135500002220.

Durham, C. D. (2004) "Timuel D. Black, Bronzeville's Venerable Historian." Hyde Park Historicial Society: Chicago, Ill.

Manheim, F. T., and E. Hellmuth. (July 2006). "Sumner and Lincoln High Schools: Black Schools that Dominated Science Awards in Greater Kansas City During the Decade of *Brown v. Board of Education*." http://www.sciencespectrumonline.com/artman/publish/printer_150.shtml (accessed March 21, 2010).

Peavler, D. J. (2005). "Drawing the Color Line in Kansas City: Creation of Sumner High School." *Kansas History: A Journal of the Central Plains*. 27 (Autumn 2005): 188–201.

Wang, R. (May 27, 2008). "Posted." *Captain Walter Dyett*. http://www.chicagojazz.com/thescene/captain-walter-dyett-86.html (accessed January 10, 2010).

UNPUBLISHED ARTICLES

Boone, W. W. (1986). "A History of Black Education in Kansas City, Kansas: Reading,

Riting, Rithemic." *U.S.D 500*. Kansas City, Kansas Board of Education.

Davis, Scottie P. (1935). "The History of Sumner High School." Student writers/editors: L. J. Franklin, E. Brewer, A. Davis, B. L. Ellis, O. Kelley, and L. E. Calhoun. (Class of 1935). (prize-winning project).

NEWSPAPERS

Kansas City Voice. The Yesterdays of Sumner. Sumner Salute Edition, June 8–June 14, 1978, 3(51).

Nordra SumCour Edition (1996). *In the Same Breath*. A Publication of the First District Economic Development Conference. Sumner High School Class of 1966. 30 Year Reunion. July 1996.

SUMNER COURIER

May 1920, 1(6)

November 15, 1920, 1(2)

December 1, 1920, 2(3)

December 15, 1920, 2(4)

February 1, 1921, 2(6)

May 16, 1921, 2(10)

October 17, 1921, 3(1)

November 15, 1921, 3(2)

January 16, 1922, 3(4)

February 15, 1922, 3(5)

November 15, 1923, 4(1 and 2)

January 31, 1924, 4(3)

October 14, 1936, 14(1)

January 31, 1947, 22(4)

November 8, 1949, 25(2)

October 12, 1950, 26(1)

May, 1951, 26(8)

January, 1953, 28(4)

March 1953, 28(6)

February, 1954, 29(7)

October, 1954, 30(1)

December 1954, 3(3)

September 20, 1963, 39(1) (*The Courier: "Voice of Spartantown"*)

January 10, 1964, 39(8)

March 11, 1964, 39(12)

October 30, 1964, 40(4)

January 14, 1966, 40(9)

March 6, 1967, 6(2)

March 12, 1967, 41(13)

March 23, 1967, 41(14)

May 3, 1967, 41(17)

May 19, 1967, 41(18)

February 8, 1968, 13(9)

December 5, 1969, 41(3)

May 18, 1972, 42 (10)

December 23, 1977, 7(3) (*Courier: Sumner High School, Kansas City, Kansas*)

April 7, 1978, 7(5)

May 19, 1978, 7(6)

May 24, 1978, 7(7) (Last school newspaper published)

ONLINE PERIODICALS

Crispus Attucks High School, Indianapolis, Indiana

"Crispus Attucks High School. Library Factfiles," http://www2.indystar. com/library/factfiles/history/black_history/attucks.html, online edition of the *Indianapolis Star* (accessed November 20, 2009).

Rabjohns, J. (2005). "Crispus Attucks: Champions for Change: The Big O Recalls Glory in an Age of Injustice. http://www2.indystar.com/ articles/5/225729-5435-256.html, online edition of the *Indianapolis Star* (accessed November 20, 2009).

"Crispus Attucks High School---Indianapolis: A Discover Our Shared Heritage Travel Itinerary." http://www.nps.gov/nr/travel/Indianapolis/crispusattaucks.htm (accessed November 20, 2009).

"Crispus Attucks High School." http://en.wikipedia.org/wiki/Crispus Attucks High School (accessed November 20, 2009).

"Crispus Attucks High School." *Historical Marker Database.* http://www. hmdb.org/marker.asp?marker=1847 (accessed November 20, 2009).

Davis, R. L. F. (2004). "Creating Jim Crow: In-Depth Essay from the History of Jim Crow." http://www.jimcrowhistory.org/history/Creating2.htm.

Frederick Douglass High School, Baltimore, Maryland

"Douglass Senior High School (Baltimore, MD)." http://en.wikipedia.org/ wiki/Frederick Douglass Senior High School(Baltimore, Maryland) (accessed August 31, 2009).

"Douglass Senior High School. Public School Review." http://www. publicschoolreview.com/school_ov/school_id/35876 (accessed August 31, 2009).

Genzlinger, N. (2008). "A High School Finds Itself Left Behind and Drowning." *New York Times.* http://www.nytimes.com/2008/06/23arts/television/23high.html (accessed August 31, 2009).

Paul Lawrence Dunbar (circa 1890). "Today in History. June 27. Paul Lawrence Dunbar." http://lcweb2.loc.gov/ammen/today/June 27.html (accessed August 27, 2009).

"Upper Marlboro Maryland School Ratings—Public and Private." http:// www.greatschools.net/city/upper_Marlboro/MD (accessed August 31, 2009).

Dunbar High School (Baltimore, Maryland)

Brown, M. "Douglass High School." *Essays by Mandela Brown and Kenneth Griffin*. Research project funded by the Annie E. Casey Foundation. http://www.mccivilrights.org/DunbarDouglass.html (accessed August 27, 2009).

Brown, M., and K. Griffin. *Essays by Mandela Brown and Kenneth Griffin*. Research project funded by the Annie E. Casey Foundation. http://www.mdcivilrights.org/DunbarDouglass.html (accessed August 27, 2009).

"Paul Lawrence Dunbar High School (Baltimore, MD)." http://en.wikipedia.org/wiki/Paul_Lawrence_Dunbar_High_School(Baltimore,Maryland) (accessed August 27, 2009).

Paul Lawrence Dunbar High School, Little Rock, Arkansas

Paul Lawrence Dunbar High School, Little Rock: Commemorating a Well-Preserved, Top Quality Rosenwald School. http://info.aia.org/nwsltr_hrc.cfm?pagename=hrc_a_dunbarhigh (accessed Retrieved January 5, 2010).

"Paul Lawrence Dunbar High School of Little Rock." *The Encyclopedia of Arkansas History and Culture*.

http://www.encyclopediaofarkansas.net/encyclopedia/entry-detail.asp?entryID=2859 (accessed January 11, 2010).

Dunbar High School, Washington, D.C.

"Dunbar High School." http://en.wikipedia.org/wiki/Dunbar_High_School (Washington,D.C.) (accessed August 27, 2009).

Johnson, C. *The Scurlock Studio and Black Washington: Picturing the Promise*. Smithsonian exhibition. http://blackfivesblog.com/?tag=dunbar-high-school (accessed August 27, 2009).

McQuirter, M. A. *African Americans in Washington D.C. 1800–1975*. Reprinted from Marya Annette McQuirter, *African American Heritage Trail*, Washington, D.C.: Cultural Tourism, 2003. http://www.culturaltourismdc.org/information3949/inforamtion_show.htm (accessed August 27, 2009).

DuSable High School, Chicago, Illinois

"DuSable High School." http://en.wikipedia.org/wiki/DuSable_High_School (accessed November 20, 2009).

"DuSable High School." *Public School Review.* http://www.publicschoolreview. com/school_ov/school_id/24029 (accessed November 20, 2009). from

Huntington High School, Newport News, Virginia

"Collis P. Huntington High School." http://en.wikipedia.org/wiki/Collis_P. Huntington_High_School (accessed January 1, 2010).

"Huntington High School—Quick Facts." *Virginia African American Heritage Sites & Organizations.* http://www.aaheritageva.org/search/sitesphp?site_id=605 (accessed August 31, 2009).

A. H. Parker High School, Birmingham, Alabama

"A. H. Parker High School." http://en.wikipedia.org/wiki/A.H._Parker_High_ School (accessed September 1, 2009).

United Alumni Association. "A. H. Parker High School History." http:// parkerslumni.com/history.htm (accessed September 1, 2009).

Charles Sumner High School, St. Louis, Missouri

"Sumner High School (St. Louis)." http://en.wikipedia.org/wiki/Sumner_ High_School_(St._Louis) (accessed July 22, 2009).

Sumner Alumni

Banks, Lacy. "Conquering Cancer and Heart failure." Chicago Sun-Times. October 2008. March 10, 2010. http://www.blogs.suntmes.com/banks/2008/10/ my_best_friend_has_died_and_i.html

Bowers, Brent. "Are You ready to Start Your Own Business." AARP, The Magazine. June 2007. March 26, 2010. http://www.aarpmagazine.org/money/ head_for_business.html?print=yes.

Buckener, Reginald T. (1982) A History of Music Education in the Black Community of Kansas City, Kansas, 1905-1954. *The Journal of Research in Music Education,* 30(2), 91-106.

Cizik, Richard. "Statement of national Association of Evangelicals." Worldwide Faith News. September 2001. March 26, 2010. http://www.wfn.org/2001/09/msg00089.html.

Dillon, Sam. " U.S Data show Rapid Minority Growth in Schools Rolls." New York Times.com. August 24, 2009. http://www.nytimes.com/2007/06/01/education/01educ.html?_r=1.

"Entrepreneurs Speakers Program." Institue for Entrepreneurship and Innovation. July 2009. http://entrepreneurhip.bloch.umkc.edu/beyondclassroom/ronaldharland.asp.

Gardner, Christine J. "Evangelicals: Power in Unity." Christianity Today. April 2000. March 26, 2010. http://www.christianitytoday.com/ct/2000/april24/16.25.html.

Mereday, Meta. "MBE Leadership." Spearman Enterprises. March 26, 2010. http://www.seonline.biz/pr07.htm.

"Minnesota man named SBA exporter of the year." Small Business Administraion. May 1991. July 2008. www.http://findarticles.com/p/articles/mi_m1052/is_n9_v112/ai_10737682.

REPORT

State Department of Education and North Central Accreditation *Self-Evaluation of Sumner High School 1968–1969.*

BUY A SHARE OF THE FUTURE IN YOUR COMMUNITY

These certificates make great holiday, graduation and birthday gifts that can be personalized with the recipient's name. The cost of one S.H.A.R.E. or one square foot is $54.17. The personalized certificate is suitable for framing and will state the number of shares purchased and the amount of each share, as well as the recipient's name. The home that you participate in "building" will last for many years and will continue to grow in value.

Here is a sample SHARE certificate:

HABITAT FOR HUMANITY

THIS CERTIFIES THAT

<u>YOUR NAME HERE</u>

HAS INVESTED IN A HOME FOR A DESERVING FAMILY

1985-2005

TWENTY YEARS OF BUILDING FUTURES IN OUR COMMUNITY ONE HOME AT A TIME

1200 SQUARE FOOT HOUSE @ $65,000 = $54.17 PER SQUARE FOOT
This certificate represents a tax deductible donation. It has no cash value.

YES, I WOULD LIKE TO HELP!

I support the work that Habitat for Humanity does and I want to be part of the excitement! As a donor, I will receive periodic updates on your construction activities but, more importantly, I know my gift will help a family in our community realize the dream of homeownership. **I would like to SHARE in your efforts against substandard housing in my community!** *(Please print below)*

PLEASE SEND ME _____ SHARES at $54.17 EACH = $ $_____

In Honor Of: _____

Occasion: (Circle One)   HOLIDAY   BIRTHDAY   ANNIVERSARY

      OTHER: _____

Address of Recipient: _____

Gift From: _____ *Donor Address:* _____

Donor Email: _____

I AM ENCLOSING A CHECK FOR $ $_____ PAYABLE TO HABITAT FOR HUMANITY OR PLEASE CHARGE MY VISA OR MASTERCARD *(CIRCLE ONE)*

Card Number _____ Expiration Date: _____

Name as it appears on Credit Card _____ Charge Amount $ _____

Signature _____

Billing Address _____

Telephone # Day _____ Eve _____

PLEASE NOTE: Your contribution is tax-deductible to the fullest extent allowed by law.
Habitat for Humanity • P.O. Box 1443 • Newport News, VA 23601 • 757-596-5553
www.HelpHabitatforHumanity.org